WINDS OF
CHANGE

WINDS OF CHANGE

Myth and Truth in Feng Shui and BaZi

ALAN CHONG KIN MENG
AU YONG CHEE TUCK

PARTRIDGE

Copyright © 2016 by Alan Chong Kin Meng.
Au Yong Chee Tuck - Contributing Editor

ISBN:	Hardcover	978-1-4828-6538-7
	Softcover	978-1-4828-6537-0
	eBook	978-1-4828-6539-4

Because of the dynamic nature of the Internet, any web addresses or links contained in this book may have changed since publication and may no longer be valid. The views expressed in this work are solely those of the author and do not necessarily reflect the views of the publisher, and the publisher hereby disclaims any responsibility for them.

Print information available on the last page.

To order additional copies of this book, contact
Toll Free 800 101 2657 (Singapore)
Toll Free 1 800 81 7340 (Malaysia)
orders.singapore@partridgepublishing.com

www.partridgepublishing.com/singapore

CONTENTS

FOREWORD
BY ALAN CHONG

When I first became interested in Chinese metaphysics, my first love was and remained the study of *feng shui*. Later, during the journey of learning, I also studied other ancillary subjects such as *Qi Men Dun Jia, Ba Zi* and palmistry.

How quickly the years have passed! It seemed almost like half a lifetime of learning.

Perhaps I have been more fortunate than most because along the arduous path of learning, I met many *feng shui* masters who were willing to teach me the authentic and genuine art of *feng shui*. Otherwise, if I had traversed the learning curve of most other students, it was very likely that I would have gleaned only half-truths from self-acclaimed masters.

If it was my good fortune to have been able to learn the lineage *feng shui* – which was entirely different from non-lineage *feng shui* – then perhaps it was only fitting that I should repay the debt to society. Probably one of the more effective ways to do this might be to write my maiden book on *feng shui*.

I have been in the industry long enough to find that the *feng shui* industry seemed to have gradually degenerated into some sort of miniature circus. This is a rather melancholic state of affairs.

In the society of ancient China, the *feng shui* master was a full time practitioner seeking to earn his living from his skills. A few masters have even eschewed the pursuit of material wealth. Instead, they preferred to probe the true secrets of *feng shui* and help their clients to resolve their issues in life.

However, some practitioners tended to use fear tactics to scare the unsuspecting public to part with their hard earned money. Other practitioners have even gone further by exploiting young and vulnerable women who were looking for a potential husband.

In the *feng shui* industry, these unscrupulous practitioners were known as Jiang Wu. The term Jiang Wu referred to the society within which they existed to earn their living. These practitioners of bad repute have no lineage; they frequently mixed liberal doses of religious or cultural practices into their *feng shui*.

After China was compelled to open up to the West in the late 1800s and early 1900s, the practice – but not necessarily the authentic knowledge – of *feng shui* slowly spread to the Westerners.

As a result, two new and distinct groups of *feng shui* practitioners evolved. One group could be loosely classified as those who learnt *feng shui* by themselves, usually by reading books. They might also have augmented their knowledge by attending seminars whose content had been simplified and toned down for the masses. This group could be loosely described as the happy week-end *feng shui* warriors who acquired their understanding largely on a do-it-yourself basis.

Despite their interest in the subject, they seemed oblivious to the fact that many books contained some degree of error. Therefore, reading more books on the subject did not necessarily increase their knowledge. The errors inherent in one book might have been repeated by another writer in the other book. Sometimes these errors were even repeated in the numerous books written by the same author!

When what was untrue was repeated too often, one day it would become a historical fact.

The other group comprised of Western educated, non-lineage *feng shui* practitioners. As they were strongly influenced by Western values and perspectives, they relied heavily on Western marketing methods to display their *feng shui* knowledge.

However, the presence of superficial *feng shui* practitioners did not imply that there were no genuine *feng shui* masters in the industry.

As far as the layman was concerned, how could he know whether the self-acclaimed *feng shui* master was really the master that he claimed to be?

If the proof of the pudding was in the eating, then perhaps the most reliable yardstick was whether the client's issues were resolved within a year or so of engaging the *feng shui* master.

If instead of progress and improvement, the client found that his situation deteriorated even further, then that showed the *feng shui* master could not deliver the promised results. The sad part was that by the time the client found out the truth, he would have already parted with a considerable amount in *feng shui* fees.

Since most clients were the average wage earner or businessman who had to struggle to earn a living and support his family, it was heart breaking to hear stories within the industry that the *feng shui* master that they had engaged had only made their condition worse.

One inevitable result from this fall out was that many laymen would eventually become wary of *feng shui* in general and *feng shui* masters in particular.

It would be a sad day when the general public dismissed the art of *feng shui* as fake hocus pocus due to their bad experiences with *feng shui* practitioners.

We have endeavoured to share our perspectives and experiences here with our readers and explain what is authentic and what is not genuine in *feng shui* and *Ba Zi*.

PART ONE
INTRODUCTION TO FLYING STARS FENG SHUI

What is *feng shui*?

We live in a modern, connected, digital, shrinking world. Yet after centuries of advances in science and technology, there are people who seemed to pick up their ears at the mention of *feng shui*.

In the West, people generally tended to have a scientific bent of mind. They wanted proof of this or that phenomena. They would not accept things at face value. After all, they had put Man on the moon and had even begun probes on Mars.

But there has been an increasing trend of people in the West who began to accept *feng shui* despite the lack of so called hard "evidence." Some evidence of this trend may be found in the increasing number of books and online articles about *feng shui*.

This brought us to the question, why should people be interested in an esoteric subject like *feng shui*?

We suggest that one probable reason was that *feng shui* had the potential to change a person's destiny.

But could *feng shui* really change our destiny? Or was it merely clever marketing hype?

If *feng shui* was practised by a competent practitioner, it could bring about benefits to the client in terms of wealth, health, academic luck and descendants' luck.

Conversely, if the *feng shui* job was bungled by a hack practitioner, then it could also cause disaster to the family members.

The basic concept of *feng shui* was that the world comprised of energies. The components of this energy can be affected by several factors. There is ample scientific evidence that there is cosmic energy, magnetic fields in the earth, tectonic plate movements, the energy of the changing winds and tides. All of these phenomenon can affect the energy field or the composition in Nature.

The *feng shui* practitioner usually spent his lifetime trying to understand how the *Qi* or energy and how to harness it for the benefit of his clients.

The *Qi* may be neutral but it affected, for better or worse, the occupants of the property. Even if a person did not believe in the existence of *Qi*, the energy was there and it affected him.

For instance, a person did not have to believe that there was gravity. But gravitational fields were there and it had some bearing on us, whether or not we cared about it.

Although *feng shui* had the potential to affect our luck, it still required human effort on our part to bring about the benefits.

Feng Shui changes our luck just like us having a better vehicle but Man decides its effectiveness because man is the master of his own destiny.

The principal method of *feng shui* that we shall use in this book will be the system known as Xuan Kong Flying Star *feng shui*.

Xuan Kong Flying Stars

It is one of the most potent *feng shui* methods used for the dwellings of living persons, whether the buildings were for commercial or residential purposes. If the student were to learn and apply this methodology, it would usually take several years because after he has learnt it, he has to apply it in practice. However, since this book was written for the beginners, we shall merely explain some basic concepts here so that the new reader might understand better some of the technicalities involved in our articles.

Xuan Kong Flying Star (or Flying Stars, for short) was part of the San Yuan School of *feng shui*. The Flying Stars were based on the nine stars of the north ladle. The nine stars were known as Tan Lang, Ju Men, Lu Cun, Wen Chu, Lian Zhen, Wu Qu, Po Chun, Zuo Fu and You Bi respectively. Each star had its own characteristics and was also assigned a number.

Star	Name	Colour	Element
1	Tan Lang	White	Water
2	Ju Men	Black	Earth
3	Lu Cun	Green	Wood
4	Wen Qu	Green	Wood
5	Lian Zhen	Yellow	Earth
6	Wu Qu	White	Metal
7	Po Chun	Brown Red	Metal
8	Zuo Fu	White	Earth
9	You Bi	Purple	Fire

For the benefit of our Western readers, sometimes the names of these nine stars have been translated as shown in the table below.

Star	Name	Translation
1	Tan Lang	Greedy Wolf
2	Ju Men	Huge Door
3	Lu Cun	Rank or Rewards
4	Wen Qu	Literary Arts

5	Lian Zhen	Chastity or Honesty
6	Wu Qu	Military Arts
7	Po Chun	Broken Army
8	Zuo Fu	Left Assistant
9	You Bi	Right Assistant

For instance, star 4 was Wen Qu so if this star was present in the landform of the mountains (or Dragons), then it could be said to benefit people whose occupation involved writing. These persons need not be full time professional fiction writers but could also encompass professors in the universities or practising doctors who wrote medical treatises.

Lo Shu

The Lo Shu was a pattern of the nine numbers arranged in a unique way. According to legend, this set of numbers was first discovered by King Wen.

The most significant contribution of the Lo Shu to Flying Stars was the location of the numbers and the arrangement of these numbers within the nine squares.

4	9	2
3	5	7
8	1	6

Together with the Lo Shu and the nine stars, they formed the Earth Plate of the Luo Pan.

Landforms

In the Book of Burial, *feng shui* was defined as harnessing auspicious *Qi*. In the Chinese context, *Qi* could be considered as a form of energy. Examples of landforms were mountain ranges, hills, rivers, lakes and the sea. Each of these landforms exerted their influence on the property. The shape and location of these landforms affected the quality of the house.

Qi rides within the Winds and scatters and when it borders the water it shall be retained – Guo Pu, Zhang Shu

Thus, any authentic *feng shui* system must adhere to this concept.

Basic Terminology

The natal chart of a property can be seen in the Flying Star chart below. It consisted of nine squares; each square represented a direction except for the square in the centre. In each square, there were three numbers.

Sitting Star   Facing Star
Period Number

The **Sitting** star represented the human factors and it reacted with mountains.

The **Facing** star represented the wealth factors and it reacted with water features.

The **Period Number** of the Heaven Plate represented the time factor of the property.

Period

The term Period was used to refer to a given time frame. Each Period was valid for twenty years. It started from Period One until Period Nine, after which the cycle was repeated.

Three Periods made up one Cycle. Therefore, since each Period consisted of twenty years, one complete Cycle would encompass sixty years.

As we can see from the table show below, the year 2016 indicated that we were currently in Period Eight.

Period	Year
One	1864 - 1883
Two	1884 - 1903
Three	1904 - 1923
Four	1924 - 1943
Five	1944 - 1963
Six	1964 - 1983
Seven	1984 - 2003
Eight	2004 - 2023
Nine	2024 - 2043

Timing of Qi

The concept of time was vital to Flying Stars *feng shui* because it would tell us whether the *Qi* was timely or out of timing.

If the *Qi* was timely, it was known as Prosperous *Qi* or Rising *Qi*. If it was out of timing, the *Qi* was known as Destructive *Qi*, Retreating *Qi* or even Dead *Qi*.

When *Qi* was timely, it was considered as auspicious *Qi*. It would bring about beneficial results in terms of wealth or human relationships for the occupants of the given property.

If *Qi* was untimely, it could cause unfavourable events such as arguments, loss of wealth, divorce, dull people, sickness and accidents.

Since we are currently in Period Eight, the timely stars were 8 and 9. The untimely or expired stars were 2, 5 and 7.

The stars which were timely or out of timing would change from one Period to another.

A word of caution: Please do **NOT** *try to do Do-It-Yourself feng shui without proper supervision or guidance.*

Plotting the House Natal Chart

The purpose of drawing up the natal chart of a property was to tell us the type of *Qi* or energy that was present in that property. From the natal chart, an experienced practitioner could determine where the auspicious *Qi* was and then work out how to utilise it for wealth, human relationships or health.

In order to draw the natal chart, we needed to determine the following:-

1. The Period number of the property.
2. The Facing of the property.
3. The compass reading of the property direction by using the Luo Pan or *feng shui* compass

It may seem rather straightforward but in practice, students sometimes got one or more of these factors wrong. If any one or more of these factors were wrong, obviously we would end up with an erroneous chart. This would result in the wrong reading and wrong solution given to the client.

SE		S		SW
3 4 7	8 8 3	1 6 5
2 5 6	4 3 8	6 1 1
7 9 2	9 7 4	5 2 9
NE		N		NW

Illustration of Flying Star Chart of a Sitting Zi (子) Facing Wu (午)

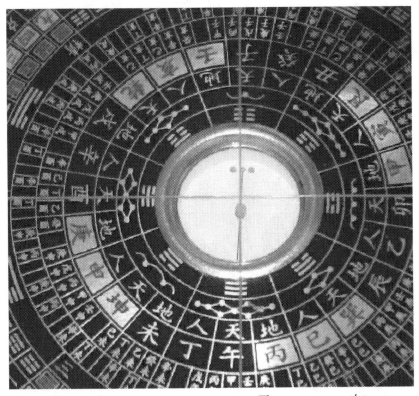

Illustration of Luo Pan Sitting Zi (子) Facing Wu (午)

The Luo Pan was the fundamental tool of the *feng shui* practitioner. It consisted of the Heaven's Pool which was the needle designed to point to the south.

There was also a round plate which turned around like a turntable. This plate contained the formulae used by any particular school of *feng shui*. Therefore, each school would design this circular plate in a different way.

The utmost care must be taken in the handling of the Luo Pan in order to take an accurate reading. If there was an error of even one degree, it would affect the reading. In turn, this would affect the analysis and diagnosis of the property.

Why did we need to use a Luo Pan? From the scientific perspective, there are geomagnetic stresses within the earth. The Luo Pan was designed to measure these geomagnetic stresses. The geomagnetic stress influenced the type of *Qi* that entered the property. That explained why a row of terrace houses facing the same direction had different qualities in terms of *feng shui*.

The Prediction Tool

Flying star *feng shui* has the strong ability to predict events in the property. One of the predictive tool is known as the 81 combinations. This is read collectively the pair of Sitting Star and Facing Star together.

For example, 2-3 is known to cause arguments & loss of wealth, 6-7 can cause accidents, 4-6 may cause occupants to commit suicide from hanging while 8-9 is happy events.

Essentially, any complete *feng shui* system must have the ability to predict but this has also led to some practitioners viewing flying star as a divination *feng shui* for solely prediction purposes only. This is a rather misconstrued view.

Classification of *Feng Shui*

Generally speaking, there are two types of *feng shui*. The Yang *feng shui* dealt with properties for living persons. These properties included residential buildings such as houses and apartments; commercial buildings such as shops, offices, shopping malls, factories and even hospitals.

The Yin *feng shui* dealt with properties for the deceased such as burial plots, life graves and ancestral tablets.

To put it another way, the Yang *feng shui* dealt with buildings built above the ground whereas Yin *feng shui* was concerned with properties located under the ground (except ancestral tablets).

What is truly *feng shui?*

If most people who had no training in *feng shui* were asked to list down what they thought *feng shui* was all about, they might include some of the following items:-

1. It involved living in harmony with nature.
2. It was all about the art of placement of furniture and objects.
3. It was part and parcel of interior design.
4. It was about space cleansing.
5. It was about decorating the property with good luck charms and symbols.
6. It was about placing items to enhance the wealth, especially in commercial properties
7. It was about ensuring that the number of the house or street was a lucky number.
8. It was about counting how many steps there were in the staircase.

All of these were common fallacies. As if that was not enough, here are some more widespread myths about *feng shui.*

1. If he lived near the cemetery, it would invite disaster.
2. If he lived near to places of worship such as temples or churches, it would bring bad luck.
3. If the front door faced directly towards the back door, it was leak of wealth.
4. The Ba Gua mirror could be used to deflect bad luck.
5. The person who lived in a high rise apartment would be less lucky than the person who lived in a landed property.
6. If he slept with his legs facing the door, it would be unlucky.
7. If he slept in a bed that was located behind the wall of a stove, it would bring health issues.
8. If he sat with a wall behind him, he would receive support at work and at home.
9. If there was a toilet located above the main door, it was a bad omen.
10. If there were dead plants in the wealth corner, it would lead to loss of wealth.
11. If the property had a hill behind for backing and faced the sea, it was an auspicious property.
12. If he could read the landforms in the vicinity of his property, it was sufficient to deduce whether the property was auspicious.

These fallacies and myths had nothing to do with the proper study of authentic *feng shui*. Contrary to common belief, *feng shui* was not a religion or tied down to any religious or cultural beliefs.

In order to derive the benefits from auspicious *feng shui*, it would require some time to take effect. In the meantime, the client would be well advised to take appropriate human action to get the desired results.

Chapter One
SMALL PROPERTY, PROSPEROUS RESULTS

In the current economic scenario, it would not be an exaggeration to say that the average income earner living in the sprawling Klang valley of Malaysia could probably not afford to buy a landed property. In the case of a married couple, even assuming that both partners were working, they would still find that they could not afford to buy even a modest single storey terrace house in the suburbs.

TAKING THE PLUNGE (GULP!) TO BUY AN APARTMENT

It was little wonder then that most couples settled to buy an apartment. In early 2010, the year of the 庚寅 Geng Yin (Metal Tiger), that was precisely what Kate (not her real name) and her husband, William (not his real name, either!) decided to do.

After some initial survey and consideration, they took the plunge and paid the down payment for a three room apartment in the bustling Kuchai Lama area of Kuala Lumpur. The apartment had a built up area of about 1,000 square feet which meant that it was only a modest size unit for what was then a family of five.

Their unit was located on the twelfth floor of the block. The first four floors were used as parking lots and the residential units started only from the fifth floor.

At that period of their lives, their income was uncertain. They were more likely to be short of money rather than have a surplus at the end of the month. The husband was sometimes unemployed and there seemed to be no certainty that he could find gainful employment anytime soon.

Their future prospects, if not exactly bleak, were not necessarily encouraging either!

WHY YOU SHOULD NOT BUY AN APARTMENT – ACCORDING TO *FENG SHUI*

It has been said by some *feng shui* masters that the owners of a landed property would benefit much more than the occupants of an apartment or condominium. They argued that the landed property retained its contact with the ground, thereby gaining the benefit of the earth *Qi* or energy. By definition, an apartment had to be away from the ground.

They further argued that an apartment owner would have to "share" his good *feng shui* (if indeed there was any) with all the other owners of the remaining units in his block. If one block had twelve floors with ten unit per floor, that would work to 120 owners. If we did the maths, then the person who owned one unit would be entitled to a mere 1/120 share of the benefits of good *feng shui* – assuming that there was any good *feng shui*, in the first place!

Other *feng shui* masters have indicated that it was more difficult to determine the facing direction of a particular apartment. For instance, should one use the main door or the balcony door to work out the facing direction? Or should we go further away and use the elevator door or even the guard house because it faced the main road which in turn brought the *Qi* into the area? Of course, it followed that if the *feng shui* master could not work out the facing direction, how was he going to determine the *feng shui* of that particular unit?

If these arguments were valid, then the logical conclusion would be that people who were fortunate enough to own landed properties should always fare better economically compared to those who could only hope to own apartments.

But when we came down to the ground and made a brief random survey, we did not find this to be the case, let alone the rule.

OOPS! THIS COUPLE ACTUALLY PROSPERED AFTER BUYING THEIR APARTMENT!

How to explain the differences? For instance, in our selected case study of Kate and her husband, their financial situation improved significantly within a mere four years. The husband was given a lucrative job opportunity. After accepting the offer, he was given several promotions.

In 2012, the year of 壬辰 Ren Chen (Water Dragon), he was mildly shocked to receive a bonus because he had not been expecting any rewards.

In this year, the annual star 6 entered the centre palace and the 3 Jade star arrived at their main door. Some practitioners of conventional flying stars would consider this pattern as an argument year.

5	1	3
4	6	8
9	2	7

2012 Flying Star Chart

MARK AND ANTONY

In the meantime, their children began to show better results in their examinations.

The elder son, Mark, was the more serious one who paid more attention to his studies. Recently, he managed to become the top dog (or rather, top student) in his class.

The younger son, Antony, was rather more playful. But lately, he seemed to become more focused on his studies. He was in the bottom rung of the top 100 students in his school. Gradually, he managed to climb up to the first 50 students. Lately, he reached the top 20 students.

Were there *feng shui* factors in play? To the casual observer, it might seem a random event. But some of our readers who had some degree of familiarity with *feng shui,* there was cause and effect.

The apartment benefitted from auspicious academic *Qi.* As if this was not enough, the human factor was further strengthened by the mountain dragon.

THE EXTERNAL AND THE INTERNAL OF *FENG SHUI*

In the study of *feng shui,* there are two major components. The first part was to survey the external landforms of a given area. This analysis would consider the water and mountain features of that area.

For instance, we would have to take into account where the river was located and which direction it flowed towards. In an urban environment, the river might not be so visible because it could be blocked from view. Nevertheless, a river out of sight did not necessarily mean that it did not exist. Alternately, we could also consider the road formations as the "river" bringing the *Qi* to that area.

The second component in analysing *feng shui* was the interior of the building, whether landed property or an apartment.

We would take the facing direction of the block as a starting point. Then we would measure the facing direction of the apartment based on the main door of that particular unit.

The unit that Kate and her spouse bought was seated on the South. If it was seated on the South (or fire), that meant it faced North (or water).

Now that we have worked out the facing direction (which seemed to be a difficult issue for those *feng shui* practitioners who argued against purchasing apartments), we could observe the external land forms.

At the rear of their unit was a hill. In the front of the same unit was a wide space. In feng shui terms, this wide space was deemed to be a *Ming Tang* or Bright Hall which served to collect the *Qi.*

When we stood outside the property, facing outwards, the right side was known as the White Tiger and the left side was called the Green Dragon. In theory, the Green Dragon or left side should be higher than the White Tiger, or right side.

In this particular case, there was no embrace between the White Tiger and the Green Dragon. If we stuck to the theory of *feng shui*, then the lack of embrace should have resulted in the leak of *Qi*. In that case, how could we explain why the luck of the couple improved after they purchased the property?

The main issue was that their unit received both *Promoting Qi* and *Auspicious Qi*. When a property benefitted from these types of *Qi*, the occupants would prosper.

In addition, their stove was located in the suitable location. This feature would result in a harmonious family life. The couple became less stressful and began to lead healthier lives.

WHAT TO DO IF YOU COULD NOT AFFORD TO BUY LANDED PROPERTY?

This real life example showed that it was not essential to buy a landed property to enjoy prosperity.

Even if the theory of *feng shui* that landed property was better than apartments was valid, in practice, we would do well to remember that the cost of landed property is so exorbitant, that the man in the street could *not* afford to buy even a modest landed property.

In that event, should we deduce that the average income earner (read, the working class) would be doomed never to be able to enjoy some good *feng shui* all their lives?

LESSON LEARNT TO TAKE HOME

"Size does not matter in Feng Shui" — Alan Chong

We would argue that good *feng shui* is available in many locations. It was possible for even the common people to benefit from *feng shui*. It was not dependent on how close the property was to the ground or how huge the property was.

However, in order to understand how *feng shui* worked, it was necessary to have some working knowledge of *Qi*, where the *Qi* came from and how to retain the *Qi*.

Chapter Two
BIG PROPERTY, POOR RESULTS

In October 1994, business writers Jim Collins and Jerry Porras published their book, *"Built to Last."* It revealed the results of their research of eighteen companies and explained in detail why these companies were successful and visionary.

The book created a good deal of interest among corporate circles when it was first released. Sadly, with the passage of time, most of the companies that made their "A" list have suffered various degrees of decline. Critics were also quick to point out that there were many flaws when it came to listing out the characteristics of what made companies successful.

For instance, Motorola has fallen so far behind in their industry that it has long been disregarded as a front runner in the hand phone business. Sony has a long history of struggling to remain profitable. Disney has been overtaken, to some degree, by Pixar and Lucas Films. The auto giant, Ford, had a long and proud history but it has lost some its lustre to the Japanese motor competitors.

"BUILT TO LAST?"

Be that as it may, when it came to the design and construction of a shopping mall, then the mall had to become profitable and remain so in the longer term. After all, it required immense capital outlay to build the mall. It would take several years, at the minimum, before the major stakeholders could recover their cost and make some adequate profit. In that sense, the mall had to be built to last.

Given this scenario, it might be reasonable to expect that the owners of a shopping mall had given some consideration to *feng shui* factors when they designed their mall. In practice, the sad reality was that there are many shopping malls that suffered from poor business.

For instance, Phoenix Plaza which was in the Cheras suburbs, the southern part of Kuala Lumpur, had been struggling for many years. At the time of writing, it has given up the ghost, have undergone major renovation to give it a new lease of life.

IN THE BEGINNING, THERE WAS HOPE

Let us discuss why one mall had a good beginning but later declined and had to struggle to stay relevant.

This mall was built in the mid-1990s. The owners chose a good location, beside the major busy thoroughfare of Jalan Loke Yew. In the same area, there were also several main arterial roads leading to the major suburb of Cheras and the vital junction town of Kajang. There were no other major malls in the immediate vicinity. The nearest competing malls were in the bustling Bukit Bintang area, a major tourist and shopping destination. Therefore, if location was the prerequisite factor, it could be argued that the new mall owners had already scored in round one.

The mall could have had the benefit of the Kerayong River flowing beside it. This river flowed from the Ampang area down to the Royal Malaysian Air Force base (RMAF) base at Sungai Besi which was in their neighbouring area. In the study of *feng shui*, the presence of water such as a river was said to represent wealth.

However, the result was very different from the theory. The anchor tenant suffered from continual declining sales and they finally shifted out in 2000, the year of 庚辰 Geng Chen (Metal Dragon).

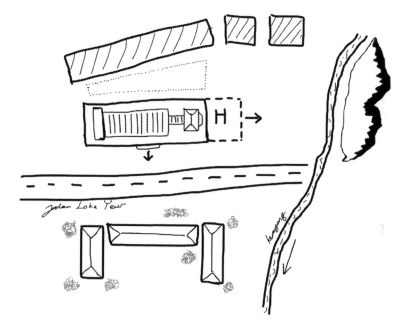

ENTER THE DRAGON

When an anchor tenant decided to leave, it naturally gave cause for concern with the mall owners. They belatedly realized the need for a *feng shui* audit and eventually hired the expertise of a well-known *feng shui* practitioner from outside the capital metropolis of Kuala Lumpur.

One of the main recommendations of this *feng shui* master was to install a fake door on the first floor in order to pull in the auspicious *Qi* or energy. It was called a fake door because while it looked like a door, complete with door handles, it was actually a window pane.

The mall underwent a sea change in late 2010 the year of 庚寅 Geng Yin (Metal Tiger). The mall owners refurbished their mall. They managed to attract new tenants such as a hypermarket, a huge Cineplex with nine screens, several banks and retail outlets selling audio visual entertainment products. The mall owners were trying to position their mall as a home entertainment and lifestyle mall to pull in the badly needed crowds.

EXIT THE TENANTS

Sadly, it was all in vain. Five years later, most of the tenants had left. Those tenants who remained behind had only few customers daily.

Ironically, in the same year of 2010 that the new management took over the shopping mall, they also constructed a hotel beside the mall. This hotel commenced operations in late 2012, the year of 壬 辰 Ren Chen (Water Dragon). The hotel was built perpendicular or at a 90 degree angle to the shopping mall. It was ironical because the hotel had good business with high occupancy rate whereas the mall's business had not improved. The mall could survive but the motor and human traffic were rather low.

The other irony was that the front door of the hotel almost directly faced the rear door. The distance between these two doors was about a hundred feet. In the *feng shui* industry, it was commonly said to be taboo for the main door to face the back door. When this situation occurred, the *Qi* was deemed to enter and exit the property so no *Qi* could be retained within the building. Within the *feng shui* industry, experts described this phenomena as *Qi* leaking.

If this theory was valid, why did the business of the hotel boom? Besides the high occupancy rate, there were also many notable public functions held at the hotel.

If two commercial properties were located in the same vicinity, they should share the same landforms. Why was it that the hotel's business prospered while the mall's business kept declining?

SAME RIVER, DIFFERENT RESULTS

The main door of the hotel faced the Kerayong River which passed from left to right. This feature brought in the auspicious *Qi* to the hotel. The main door was also placed in an auspicious sector.

The mall had a good door in a favourable location but was not able to pull in the auspicious *Qi*. Hence this weakened the wealth formation.

At the back of the mall was the car park and several high rise residential towers. The car park further activated the *Sha* and were considered to have strengthened the *Sha Qi* or destructive *Qi*.

The Kerayong River beside the mall did not bring in auspicious *Qi* to the mall. Instead, it activated more *Sha Qi*. This *Sha Qi* can cause arguments as well as bring about gradual loss of wealth for the mall.

It was a common fallacy for most people to think that wherever there was a river, there would be wealth and prosperity.

If water represented wealth, then fishermen and boat builders should be among the wealthiest segment of any society.

Instead, the shipbuilding tycoon probably lived in his mansion, located inland and far away from the sea.

LESSON LEARNT TO TAKE HOME

Two properties from the same category (that is, commercial) were located in the same location. By definition, they had to share the same landforms. Yet one commercial property fared much better than the other. How to explain the differences?

Of course, the nature of the business of each commercial property was different. This difference could have some bearing on the end result.

But the motor traffic and the commuting patterns remained the same. The practitioners of New Age *feng shui* would describe the problem of the mall as suffering from a *"wealth leaking formation"* due to the door facing door arrangement.

However, to practitioners of authentic *feng shui,* this description was considered a myth. The issues of the mall could be resolved and were fixable.

In the practice of classical *feng shui,* we tried to harness the auspicious *Qi.* But it was not advisable to play tricks on nature by installing a fake door. The art of *feng shui* was not like a magic show which produced quick fixes.

The hotel and the mall faced different directions. This would lead to entirely different results. The Kerayong River benefitted the hotel but was not favourable to the mall. This is a common fallacy where practitioners advocated the use of Landform *feng shui* without considering the building's orientation.

To non-practitioners, the fact that the anchor tenant shifted out in 2000 was a mere isolated event. For those of our readers who have some familiarity with *feng shui,* there is cause and effect.

CHAPTER THREE
LEAVE THE POT OF GOLD ALONE!

In today's fast paced world of business, it has often been said that the successful entrepreneur cannot afford to rest on his laurels. If he remained satisfied with whatever he has gained, one day his competitors will eventually overtake him and leave his company far behind. Therefore, an astute businessman should keep a sharp eye open for opportunities to exploit.

On the flip side, there have also been many true life tales of conglomerates which overreached themselves, became too heavy at the bottom or the top (such as too much senior management or too much interference from senior management) and then turned over. Some of these multinationals even ventured into other business which was not even remotely linked to their core activities.

So what should the really, genuinely shrewd businessperson do? If he expanded too fast and too far, he might overstretch his resources and become over geared. If he was contented to remain with his profitable concern, one day his company might become a gone concern.

We proposed to relate the tale of a business which did very well – until the owner decided to rent the neighbouring shop as well.

There are certain types of business where the passer by or casual customer (as differentiated from the regular customer) can observe whether or not the business is doing well.

For example, in the case of food and beverage industry or bakery and cake shop, we could easily get a rough idea that the business was good. During the peak eating hours such as lunch time, the coffee shop, fast food café or restaurant should be packed with customers.

If a cake and bread shop was located in a shopping mall, then it might be full of customers during the weekends when the mall had the most visitors.

There was a Japanese themed bakery which commenced business in a bustling commercial area about two years ago. It seemed that they already had brisk business from the word "go", that is from the first day of operations. In order to pick and choose the buns and cakes on display, we had to jostle for space among the crowd. After that, we had to join the long queue to the cashier's counter to pay for the items. If the phrase "selling like hot cakes" could be applied literally, here was a good practical example where this phrase was no cliché.

The cakes were well crafted and seemed to have the essence of the Japanese touch. As a result, they were a delight to munch and devour. Probably this was the secret of their success. If so, it certainly put them a notch or two above their competitors and left the ordinary bakeries far behind.

The shop was sitting on the North and faced the South. When we opened the main door on the right hand side, the cashier's counter was directly facing the main door with the cash register aligned a little to the left side.

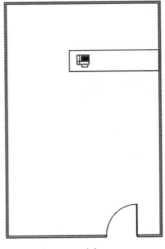

Original layout

In terms of *feng shui*, the cashier was the person who collected the takings. Therefore, his location was important because it represented the source of the income for the business.

In this case, the position of the cashier was auspicious. It was located in a favourable spot where it could receive auspicious *Qi* or energy. The layman might not be aware of this factor and thought that it was a mere coincidence. The *feng shui* practitioner would know better and realize that there was cause and effect.

There was a competing bakery in a neighbouring shop just beside this bustling bakery. Since they were in the same block, the two shops had the same facing direction which was south.

Yet despite the fact that they were in the same commercial area, even in the same block with the same facing direction, this second bakery suffered from poor business. It was impossible to estimate the ratio of customers for the two bakeries. Perhaps a haphazard guess might be that the profitable bakery could have twenty customers for every one customer that the struggling bakery had.

The neighbouring bakery offered different products and his price was also lower. The material difference was that the neighbouring competitor located the cashier's counter in a different place.

Another neighbouring shop on the other side was rented by a restaurant. After struggling for a few years, they chose to call it a day.

The prosperous bakery thought that it was a good chance to expand the business by taking over the rental of the adjacent shop. So they eventually turned it into a pastry café. The bakery was still located in the original shop but there were some inevitable changes in the layout.

Although the prosperous bakery was located nearby my residence, during the intervening period my schedule seemed to become busier. As my business activities took me far and wide, there seemed no likelihood that I would return to the shop for a bite or two.

However, there came a lull in my business turnover. At the same time, there developed a craving for the soft Japanese cheese cake.

As I strolled to the shop, I had an eerie feeling that things seemed rather quiet and deserted around the vicinity of the shop. My worst suspicions were confirmed when I reached the shop. The once bustling, jostling crowd of customers was no longer there. It seemed more like a ghost town now.

What had caused the demise of a once prosperous business concern? The immediate feature that was most striking was that the owners of the business had shifted the position of the cashier's counter to a similar arrangement as his former baker neighbour.

They had put the cashier's counter parallel to the walls of the original shop, probably to provide for more space for their shelves and display of their wares. They had hacked a small opening towards the rear of the adjoining wall of the shop. The idea was to allow the flow of their customers from the bakery to the adjacent café and vice versa.

However, in *feng shui* terms, this move was an unmitigated disaster. In the original layout, the cashier was located in an auspicious location and received beneficial *Qi*. In the revised plans, the cashier had been shifted to an inauspicious position. This new spot caused the cashier to be exposed to untimely *Qi*. This move weakened the patronage of the customers to the same extent as his former neighbouring bakery competitor.

Untimely Qi is undesirable or destructive Qi that brings about bad and unfavourable events. In short, it is bad feng shui. – Alan Chong

---

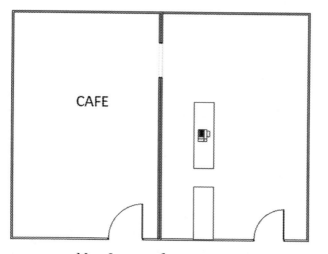

New Layout after expansion

Since I was the only customer in the shop, I had a chat with the cashier and the staff after paying for my purchases. They confirmed my initial findings. The few customers occupied only one table in the adjoining café.

How could we explain such phenomena? From the business point of view, the bakery had maintained the quality and taste of their hot selling products – except that they were no longer hot selling. They also charged the same prices as before. Yet their business had declined drastically since the business expansion.

Surely they had not made any serious mistakes from the business angle. But they had committed a serious transgression from the *feng shui* perspective when they changed the location of the cashier's counter.

To the sceptical observer, the *Qi* was an intangible object. We could not touch the energy, feel it, smell it, or even measure it. But there were also so many intangible objects in science.

For instance, Alfred Wegener proposed in 1912 that there was continental drift. Edwin Hubble showed in 1929 that there are other galaxies beyond our own galaxy. The layman may not care about these theories but the scientific community has largely accepted these theories.

To the average property owner, the *feng shui* aspect did not appear logical and might not appeal to him. It was the space in the shop or house that was visible to the owner. The issue of how to make the best usage of this space was something that the owner might want to discuss with an interior designer.

But the study of interior design had nothing in common with the study of *feng shui*. In fact, frequently the proposals of the *feng shui* practitioner clashed with the ideas of the interior designer or architect.

The competent *feng shui* practitioner was more concerned with how to determine where was the auspicious *Qi* and how to harness this auspicious *Qi* into the building.

However, the New Age *feng shui* practitioner might recommend space clearing. Sometimes, the space clearing might bring about favourable results. During the process of space clearing, we would shift our tables, wardrobes or beds. If the table or bed was shifted to an auspicious location and received good Qi, then the results would be favourable. But if the table or bed was changed to an inauspicious location, then the result would be unfavourable.

The space clearing certainly did not change or move the stagnant energy in the property. Sometimes the New Age *feng shui* practitioner did things without understanding the reasoning behind the action.

Some readers might be tempted to think that it was bad *feng shui* to rent a shop that had a previously failed business. However this was more of a myth than the truth. The reason that this new formation had not been able to benefit the tenant was due to the new cashier's position. The secondary reason was due to the enlarged space.

Enlarged space had a *Qi* changing effect that would eventually change the formation of *feng shui* of any property. Thus when one decide to extend the property, he or she must bear in mind this possible change in the *feng shui* formation.

The purpose of *feng shui* was to identify and capture auspicious Qi and minimise destructive *Qi*. The hallmark of a competent *feng shui* practitioner was to do this repeatedly so that his clients would benefit from the results. If properly practised, the effects of *feng shui* might be like hidden hands that gave us a lift or boost. If wrongly practised, the outcome might be harmful and the same hidden hands might give us a nasty drop.

The ability to tap auspicious Qi and do it repeatedly is the mastery of the Art of Feng Shui. - Alan Chong

---

At the end of the day, it was results that mattered to the clients. The practice of *feng shui* is certainly not a magic show. It was not merely a matter of showmanship or clever marketing skills to woo the audience.

CHAPTER FOUR
THE VARIOUS SCHOOLS OF FENG SHUI

Some of our readers might have attended talks on *feng shui* or have read various books on the subject. To the general reader, the topic of *feng shui* was a discipline that might be worthy of study. If he probed deeper, he would have discovered that there were many schools of *feng shui*.

This revelation might have astounded him. If *feng shui* was one subject to be studied assiduously, why should there be so many different schools? As if that was not bewildering enough, it seemed that the methods of one school of *feng shui* contradicted that of another school!

Which system then was the genuine method to get results? How did we know which was the real McCoy and which was the fake diamond?

Perhaps a meaningful answer would be what type of results we wanted to get in the first place. If we wanted to select a good grave for our ancestors, it would be very different from the selection of a shop for doing business. The ends would partly determine the means or the method.

THE TWO MAJOR TYPES OF *FENG SHUI* – THE YIN AND THE YANG

In the beginning, the practice of *feng shui* was meant to bring about benefits to the descendants of the deceased person. Therefore, this type of Yin house *feng shui* was more concerned about the selection of good burial sites and how to locate an auspicious burial ground known as the Xue (穴). *Feng shui* started with the Book of Burial authored by Guo Pu back during Jin Dynasty (AD 276 – 324). Any *feng shui* done under the ground was known as Yin house *feng shui*.

But the descendants were still alive and well. Even though the grave of their ancestor might be well designed in terms of *feng shui*, they still needed buildings to live, work and play. These buildings could range from shops, offices and factories to houses and apartments to entertainment centres such as cinemas and sport complexes. Therefore, there was demand to design good *feng shui* of buildings for the living. Any *feng shui* done above the ground, usually for buildings, was known as Yang house *feng shui*.

THE LINEAGE OF YANG YUN SUNG

Perhaps the earliest system of *feng shui* that was complete was the one complied by Master Yang Yun Sung. It was complete in the sense that there were components of both Formula as well as Landforms and these components were integrated.

Briefly speaking, and without going into great technical detail, his system was based on the 72 Dragons Formula and the three Plates. These Plates were the Earth Plate, the Man Plate and the Heaven Plate.

Master Yang was an expert on landforms because he had assiduously studied the book titled *"Book of Burial"* that was written by Guo Pu during the Jin dynasty. This book comprised of three scrolls and discussed in detail the topic of *Qi*. It was clearly stated that the source of *Qi* was derived from the mountain ranges and the bodies of water. Therefore, when *feng shui* was mentioned in this book, it referred to the art of using the *Qi* or energy of the land to benefit Man and his descendants.

There are three surviving texts written by Master Yang. These books were titled *Qing Nang Ao Yi, Tian Yu Jing* and *Yu Che Jing*.

He finally settled down in Ganzhou, China where he taught his three disciples to carry down the lineage. His high reputation as a *feng shui* master has continued up to the present times. His contributions to *feng shui* can be evidenced in his works which are still available in China.

THE *SAN HE* SCHOOLS

With the passage of time, other masters added their versions of *feng shui* based on the formulas espoused by Master Yang. These variations eventually became known as the *San He* School. It was a rather broad classification because there were many sub-schools within this group.

The *San He* method utilised the three combinations of the Twelve Earthly Branches. This would give us four types of elements which were wood, fire, metal and water.

They also used the original 72 Dragons but they added other formulae such as the 120 Tigers which was not mentioned in Master Yang's works. In the present times, some schools have produced further methods such as the *Eight Killing Roads, San He Water* method and *Five Ghost Carry Treasure*.

THE *EIGHT MANSION* SYSTEM

There was an *Eight Mansion* System that existed before the era of Master Yang. Although there were several legends about the origins of this system, it was not possible to deduce when this system began.

The most commonly accepted legend was that the Emperor ordered the monk Yi Shing to write the *Eight Mansion* method to satisfy the curiosity of commoners about *feng shui* and also to pacify the request from vassal states.

A variation on this theme was that the kingdom was invaded and the Emperor was compelled to reveal the secrets of *feng shui*. So he issued an imperial edict to the monk Yi Shing to explain how *feng shui* worked. The result was the *Eight Mansion* system, also popularly known as *Bazhai* (八宅) method.

The *Eight Mansion* system became popular because it was easy to use. It does not put much emphasis on the concept of Time. The method used the East and West group. It divided the property into eight sectors, four of which were favourable and the remainder unfavourable. Therefore, by definition, half of a given property is always inauspicious and not encouraged to be used.

This method also disregarded the passage of Time. The four favourable sectors remained favourable irrespective of which period or year the property was being analysed. Since the formula used was within the arc of 45 degrees of the compass, it was easy and safe for many practitioners to take the readings.

By breaking up the family members into two groups, East group or West group, this methodology already had the potential to cause disharmony within the family or the tribe.

XUAN KONG DA GUA SCHOOL

The *Xuan Kong Da Gua* (XKDG) system is part of the larger *San Yuan* School. They used the *San Yuan* Rings of the 24 mountains which differed significantly from the *San He* method in terms of the Yin-Yang.

The basis of the *Xuan Kong Da Gua* method was the usage of the 64 hexagrams of the *I Ching ("The Book of Changes")* which was rearranged by Shao Yong, *I Ching* scholar. A hexagram was constructed when two trigrams were mounted on each other. Each trigram had three horizontal lines. Therefore, two trigrams would comprise of six horizontal lines. The horizontal lines were also known as *Yao*. The horizontal lines could be broken or unbroken. Broken lines represents the Yin Yao while the unbroken represents the Yang Yao.

There were two major contributions to the *Xuan Kong Da Gua* system. One was made by Jing Fan who created his *Jing Fan Na Jia* method. The other came from Shao Yong who created the 64 hexagrams square encircled by a round plate, as illustrated below.

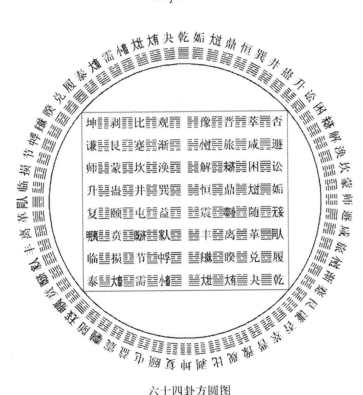

六十四卦方圆图

The other significant components about *Xuan Kong Da Gua* was that it utilised the existing landforms and placed emphasis on the effects of Time on the property. The experienced practitioner could also make some predictions using the *Xuan Kong Da Gua* method to work out the year of the event taking place.

FLYING STARS SCHOOL

The *Flying Stars* (*"Fei Xing"*) method is part of the *San Yuan* School. The basis of the system was the nine stars of the northern ladle.

Most of the texts concerning *Flying Stars* were written during the Qing dynasty so it has been disparaged by some practitioners as a relatively new method. However, this somewhat snobbish attitude only underlined their ignorance. Personally, we can testify that we had the good fortune to sight an almanac from a disciple of one *feng shui* master who was active during the Yuan dynasty (1271-1368).

Each property had a natal chart which revealed the inherent *Qi* in that property. The chart comprised of 9 squares. Inside each square there were three numbers. These were known as the Sitting Star, the Facing Star and the Period number.

The number on the top left was the Sitting Star and the number on the top right was the Facing Star. The larger number shown at the bottom and usually written in the centre of the square is the Period number. (Please refer back to the Introduction Chapter)

The Sitting Star represented the people factor while the Facing Star represented the wealth aspects.

When the two numbers were read together, they revealed many things to the experienced practitioner.

Traditionally, *feng shui* masters tried to create a balance of Yin and Yang in the property. Then there would be a balance in terms of harmonious human relationships, good health and descendant luck while also enjoying some wealth and authority.

However, with the pressure of modern living, the emphasis has shifted to the pursuit of wealth at the expense of the other factors. Due to the demands of the clients, most practitioners had to focus on the wealth factor while ignoring or downplaying the other components.

When the nine Sitting Stars were combined with the nine Facing Stars, we had a total of 81 combinations. These combinations could be used for predicting events. Since Flying Stars system was based on the San Yuan School, there was also emphasis on the time factor.

The result was that the experienced practitioner could make predictions and fine tune when these events were most likely to happen.

The occupants of some properties could enjoy good fortune only for a *feng shui* period of twenty years. But there were also a few properties which benefited its residents for more than three generations, which encompassed a time frame of several hundred years.

DRAGON EIGHT GATE SYSTEM OR *QIAN KUN GUO BAO*

The *Dragon Eight Gate* system utilised water methods. It was part of the San Yuan School. This method was very popular in Taiwan.

This system explained how the water arrived at the property, how it passed through the property and finally how it exited the property. Based solely on the entry and exit of the water, the practitioner would try to determine what were the benefits or drawbacks of the property.

OTHER NON LANDFORM BASED SCHOOLS

There are too many non-landform based schools to be explored here. Due to constraints of space and time, we shall only briefly explain some of the more common schools.

BAZI FENG SHUI

Some practitioners argued that *feng shui* should be tailored to the individual occupant of the property. The ideal way to do so was obviously to use the *Ba Zi ("Eight Character")* chart of the person to determine what type of property was most suited for him.

For instance, if the person favourable element is wood, then the practitioner suggested that the client should live in a house facing east. The reasoning was that East represented the direction for wood *Qi*.

That seemed fine in theory. But some practitioners went even further by dissecting the Yin-Yang elements in the day master.

For instance, if the client was a 丙 Bing fire day master, they recommended that he should live in an apartment because the 丙 Bing fire represented the fire of the sun. Since the sun rose high above the sky, the client should live in a high rise building. If we carried this argument to its logical conclusion, then the client's family would end up living in the penthouse!

In that regard, if the client was a 壬 Ren water day master, perhaps the practitioner should advise him to live near the sea. After all, the 壬 Ren water represented the waters of the ocean.

If there was any merit in this argument, why was it that most fishermen were not wealthy?

Another variation on this theme was to work out the useful element in the *Ba Zi* chart and make use of that element. If the useful element was the 亥 Hai (Pig), then the practitioner might recommend to open a door in the Hai sector.

The theory was fine but the application might not be so practical. If the said 丙 Bing fire day master was happily ensconced in the upper floors of his condominium block, he might not find it so easy to install a door in the 亥 Hai sector. If he did so, he might find that his auspicious door might very well open into his neighbour's unit!

My view is that *Ba Zi* is an art of Astrology and not a *feng shui* system. Astrology is used to decipher what is our destiny and the path, as reflected in the Luck cycle. Just because they use the same ten Heavenly Stems and twelve Earthly Branches, it did not necessarily mean that it could be copied wholesale into a *feng shui* system. After all, *feng shui* used mountains and bodies of water as the source of *Qi*.

ZI WEI DOU SHOU FENG SHUI

Instead of using *Ba Zi* to work out what *feng shui* was suitable for the client, the practitioner used the *Zi Wei Dou Shu ("Purple Star"* astrology) chart.

The *feng shui* practitioner would follow the *Zi Wei Dou Shu* astrology by using the nine stars of the north ladle and the lunar date and time of birth.

The practitioner would use the twelve sectors of the *Zi Wei Dou Shu* chart to divide the property into twelve sectors. Then he would advise the best sectors to use and the favourable date to shift into the property.

The concept behind this art is similar to that of *Ba Zi feng shui*.

YI JING FENG SHUI

In ancient times, *Yi Jing* was used for divination purposes. The most common method was to use yarrow stalks which were easily available. Later a method evolved whereby coins were thrown into a turtle shell. In modern times, there are even mobile apps to do the casting.

The purpose of the casting of the coins or yarrow stalks was to derive a hexagram. When this hexagram was interpreted by an experienced practitioner, he could predict events and the timing of these events. He was also required to suggest solutions to the problems that he foresaw. One method might be to produce some auspicious imagery so that the desired outcome was shown.

The *feng shui* purists would decry this method because they argued that it was better suited for divination purposes or augury. Furthermore, it used images as a source of *Qi* rather than mountains and bodies of waters.

SYMBOLISM FENG SHUI

The purpose of symbolism *feng shui* was mainly for protection but also sometimes to enhance the *feng shui* of a property.

There were numerous symbolism methods such as crystals, *Ba Gua* mirrors, *Pi Yao*, Chinese coin swords or mountain and water paintings.

The most commonly used items for protection purposes were *Ba Gua* mirrors, *Pi Yao*, *Qilin* (celestial horse) and *Fu* dogs. Other items could be wealth vase for enhancing purposes, a pair of Mandarin ducks for relationships and *Ruyi* to augment authority.

The symbolism *feng shui* was widely used by peasants for about two centuries until the Cultural Revolution in China.

In the context of modern day society, perhaps the most common example of how symbolism was used in *feng shui* involved the use of mirrors.

One well-known symbolism school of *feng shui* advocated that their client should put mirrors facing their dining table. When the family sat at the dining table to eat their meals, the mirror would reflect the food and symbolize that the quantity of food available for consumption had doubled.

However, they seemed to have forgotten to mention that the number of persons partaking the food would also have increased twofold!

If there were twice as many people eating twice the quantity of food, did that situation not bring us back to square one?

Another popular method used by symbolism *feng shui* was to put some Chinese coins of ancient design in the client's wallet or handbag. Then the money in the wallet would multiply.

In the year of the Rooster, one practitioner even advised her clients to carry eighty eight grains of rice in a plastic bag with them so that the Rooster would peck at the rice instead of at the clients!

Therefore, symbolism in *feng shui* might appeal to the layman because it was easy to understand and utilise.

CONCLUSION

The two most important methods of *feng shui* in modern times were the landform and the non-landform based methods. The debates centred on whether the non-landform based methods should deserve their place in classical *feng shui* schools. Proponents of the landform based schools argued that the non-landform based methods only gave some psychological comfort to the clients.

An authentic *feng shui* system should have these basic characteristics:-

1. Based on Landforms as source of *Qi*.
2. Usage of Luopan to determine direction of incoming energy or *Qi*.
3. The ability to predict.

CHAPTER FIVE
THE TEMPLE DIVINE

WHY WERE TEMPLES IGNORED IN *FENG SHUI?*

In the practice of *feng shui*, most masters have concentrated on designing the *feng shui* of commercial and residential buildings.

This situation was understandable. After all, most of the buildings in an urban environment were commercial or residential. Even industrial buildings such as factories were meant to be profitable and therefore, commercial oriented. And at the end of the day, even *feng shui* masters had to earn a living!

However, this gave rise to the question, could a non-commercial and non-residential building benefit from *feng shui* practices? In the first place, how could there possibly be a non-commercial and non-residential building?

If we were willing to broaden our mental horizons enough, we could find such buildings, even in the midst of the urban concrete jungle. A non-commercial building would, by definition, had to be engaged in non-profit oriented activities. The organizations whose *raison d'etre* was not to pursue wealth would have to be charitable or religious bodies.

A charitable organization such as an orphanage or home for the disabled would still require one or more buildings to house their folks. Therefore, the buildings they used would be considered as residential buildings.

But a temple was neither a commercial nor a residential building. While it was true that the monks or priests who tended to the temple still required accommodation, in most cases, they did not live inside the temple itself. They were usually housed somewhere else, perhaps in other residential buildings within the temple compound.

If a building was neither commercial nor residential, did it still require good *feng shui*? If so, what sort of *feng shui* principles should we apply? Should the *feng shui* master seek to accentuate the wealth factors or the people factors?

If he emphasized the wealth elements, the main purpose of the temple was not to pursue wealth. If he chose to enhance the human relationship angle, it might benefit the occupants of the building. There was only one minor problem. No one lived inside the temple!

Little wonder then that most *feng shui* masters did not bother with or write much material about temples!

CURIOUSITY ABOUT TEMPLES

However, the absence of such material in the already numerous and ever increasing number of books about *feng shui* intrigued this writer. He pondered long and hard about the apparent vacuum.

One day, he had the seven year itch to get up and visit the sites of various temples. During his journeys, he found a temple with superb *feng shui*.

Arguably, there were several temples that could be said to have good *feng shui*. The devotees would throng these temples during the festival days or the periods of prayer. Otherwise, the temples would be largely deserted.

THE TEMPLE OF PROSPERITY

The temple that was the subject matter of this article was bustling with devotees and visitors even during the off peak season, that is, when it was not the period for prayers. In fact, it has even been earmarked as a tourist destination. And the visitors or devotees were people who came from different ethnic backgrounds. How to explain this astounding phenomenon?

The temple was located in one of the nearby southern states from the capital metropolis, Kuala Lumpur. Some local sources indicated that this temple was built in the 1860s. That would have made the building over a hundred and fifty years old.

According to legend, the driving force behind the construction of the temple was a Taoist priest by the name of Zhong Xi Kun. Under his supervision, the materials needed for construction such as sand, bricks and pillars were carried uphill using manpower and, perhaps, some beasts of burden. After all, during that era, motor transport was still some way distant in the future. The marvel was that most of the principal structures were still solid and standing even to this day.

In order to reach this temple, we would have to travel to a quaint, quiet village. The roads to the village were narrow and winding. The temple was built on the side of a hill.

Upon reaching the site of the temple, the visitor would have to be prepared to climb a winding staircase of a few hundred steps. About halfway on his climb, he would be greeted by the sight of a fortune toad.

When the visitor finally reached the temple, he would be rewarded for his exertions by the cool breeze and a panoramic view.

THE LANDFORMS OF THE TEMPLE

The visitor can now see that the temple was located on the steep side of a hill. If he cared to take any compass directions, he would find that the rocky hills ran from the South East to the North West.

In front of the temple was a mountainous range in the north. Nestled in between these mountains was a meandering river. This river flowed towards the temple before passing by on the left side of the temple.

The visitor would be awed by the view of the huge, triangle shaped mountain that stood proudly and majestically in front of the temple.

This mountain was flanked by several smaller hills, as though it was an Imperial official surrounded by his assistants.

What effect, if any, did these landform features had on the temple? Or was it pure luck or coincidence that this auspicious site was chosen?

After all, legend has it that when the temple pioneers were searching for a suitable site, they came across a bunch of joss sticks used for praying lying on the ground. They interpreted this omen to indicate that this was an auspicious site to build their temple.

THE AUSPICIOUS *QI* THAT BENEFITTED THE TEMPLE

The river that flowed and turned from the left side to the temple strengthened the wealth for the temple. Even a non-profitable organization such as a temple needed some source of income to fund its activities. The beneficial effect of the river would be that the temple would not be short of donors and sponsors to provide for the maintenance and upkeep of the temple.

The triangle shaped mountains that stood in front of the temple indicated that there would be fame and recognition. In the study of *feng shui*, the hills represented Ren Ding or good human relationships. This helped the temple to gain fame and benefit from frequent and repeated visits from devotees.

When the mountains and rivers combined to produce auspicious results, it was little wonder why this temple excelled in human relationships and wealth matters.

WAS WEALTH OR HUMAN RELATIONSHIPS MORE RELEVANT?

If a temple had good wealth features, its coffers might usually be filled. But wealth factors alone could not be so meaningful to a religious body compared to a corporate organization.

If the focus was on wealth alone, it would be a short sighted approach to the *feng shui* of a temple. It was vital to emphasize the people factor if the temple was to continue to prosper.

Since this temple had good human relationship factors, most of the devotees would find that their prayers were usually answered. In turn, this would encourage them to return to this temple time and again. In the process, they would also spread by word of mouth about their satisfaction of coming to this temple. The end result was that there would be a continuous stream of devotees, which would arouse the curiosity of visitors to flock to the temple.

After all, this temple did not provide ancillary services such as the registration of marriages, sponsoring schools, giving talks and seminars, perhaps for a fee in return. If the temple provided only services for worshipping, then it was logical that the prayers of the devotees had to be fulfilled.

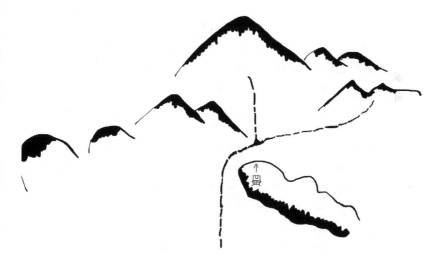

THE PROSPERITY CONTINUED

This temple had to be built with the advice of a competent *feng shui* master. The temple was able to draw in the auspicious *Qi* from the surrounding land forms. Otherwise, the presence of auspicious land forms by itself would not have been enough.

From our research, we found that even the height of the building from the ground was carefully measured. It was no accident that the temple has prospered continuously for over 150 years.

The temple already had several recently constructed pavilions beside it. At the time of writing, the temple committee had plans to build extensions. They estimated that the extensions might be completed by 2024. If these plans came to fruition, the prosperity of the temple would improve by leaps and bounds.

We have steadfastly held that the practice of *feng shui* was to harness the good *Qi* and minimize the bad *Qi*.

WHEN LUCKY CHARMS DID NOT BRING IN THE LUCK

In our view, the usage of talismans, lucky charms, holy water, putting gold coloured coins shaped like traditional Chinese coins in a person's wallet, three legged toads and Mandarin ducks were not part and parcel of traditional *feng shui*.

These were quick fixes, an easy method for Do-It-Yourself mavericks who wanted instant solutions to their issues. These good luck symbols were marketed by misinformed *feng shui* practitioners who posed as genuine *feng shui* masters out to make a quick buck. They were also came from non-lineage schools of *feng shui* masters.

In the study and practice of *feng shui*, it was vital to seek the guidance and teaching of a genuine *feng shui* master. He must have the knowledge and experience to pass on to his students. The criteria was not whether the master was known worldwide or had only a local reputation.

What is the use of a master with an international reputation but lacked the genuine knowledge or did not have sufficient experience to carry out the Yang and Yin house *feng shui* tasks?

LINEAGE IN FENG SHUI

In the tradition of teaching *feng shui*, the *feng shui* master would pass on his closely held secrets only to selected students whom he discerned as having good character and sufficient ability. From this small flock of students, he might select one or more deserving students to become his disciples. These disciples could then claim that they had some lineage descended from their master.

Therefore, in the context of *feng shui*, it was not necessary for lineage to be blood lineage or direct descendants of that particular master. Only those practitioners who did not understand or appreciate the relevance of lineage would criticize or downplay the importance of lineage.

A genuine and competent *feng shui* master would not pass down his secrets or reveal his closely held knowledge so publicly by writing innumerable books or giving countless talks. He would guard his knowledge, gained by the sweat of hard experience, as jealously as he would watch over a young and beautiful wife. The master would be willing to share his most important secrets only with his inner circle of disciples.

THE DO-IT-YOURSELF SCHOOL OF FENG SHUI

For the majority of *feng shui* students who did not have the patience or could not gain the trust of genuine *feng shui* masters, they would probably glean their knowledge of *feng shui* from the *feng shui* books that flooded the market.

While it might be possible for the curious reader to pick up a few pointers here and there, he would be left even more bewildered than before. If he read widely enough on the subject, he would have realized that what was written in one book often contradicted what was written in another book. In fact, sometimes the same writer even contradicted himself in the same book!

How then would the reader be able to separate the wheat from the chaff? The simple reply is that it was extremely dangerous to become a Do-It-Yourself *feng shui* practitioner. There was no substitute for learning this discipline from a competent *feng shui* master, usually by attending a live class and continuous practice.

"Feng shui is the art of harnessing Auspicious Qi which can be provided by the surrounding landforms." – Alan Chong.

CHAPTER SIX
THE YIN *FENG SHUI* BENEFITTED THE FEMALE DESCENDANTS

In the beginning, the study and practice of *feng shui* was concerned with the design and layout of the ancestors' graves. The Chinese have long held the view that a good ancestor grave would benefit future generations. Therefore, they paid careful attention to the selection of an auspicious grave when their ancestor passed away. There is ample evidence of this practice among the various dynasties in the history of China.

However, the proper *feng shui* method used for graves is not Flying Stars but Xuan Kong Da Gua.

THE GOOD GRAVE

We proposed to tell the tale of a prominent tycoon nearer to home, that is, in Malaysia. The father came from the southern states of the country. In the 1960s, the father passed away at a young age, when he was in his teens.

His next of kin seemed to have taken pains to ensure that he had a very good grave. When we said that it was a good grave, it had nothing to do with the size of the plot of land. Instead, we were more concerned with the landforms and the location of the grave within the memorial park or cemetery. A grave which was smaller in land size might have much better feng shui than another grave which was huge and looked grandiose.

In this particular case, the grave was located with a strong mountain formation backing it. This was important because the back of the grave was considered as the Black Tortoise. If the grave had strong backing, then there would be a supply of strong *Qi* or energy to the grave.

In the front of the grave was a vast area of flat land. This was known as the *Ming Tang* or Bright Hall. The purpose of the *Ming Tang* is for the *Qi* to accumulate. The *Ming Tang* is often symbolized to be the Phoenix. The reason was that the Phoenix will fly around in the same fashion as how the *Qi* would accumulate in front of the tomb. This is one of the reasons why many Chinese tombs have a huge open courtyard in front of the tombs.

However, the presence of the *Ming Tang* alone was not enough. If the *feng shui* practitioner was not careful, the *Qi* could still disperse from the *Ming Tang*. In the event that the *Qi* dispersed, the result would be disaster and calamity for the descendants.

THE GREEN DRAGON AND THE WHITE TIGER

Therefore, we needed two other features to enclose the *Ming Tang* and prevent the *Qi* from escaping. These features were known as the Green Dragon and the White Tiger.

When we stand in front of the grave, facing the tombstone, the Green Dragon is always on our left side. The White Tiger is always on the right hand side.

The Green Dragon is said to represent the male while the White Tiger represented the female. If the White Tiger was higher than the Green Dragon, then the effect was that the female descendants would benefit more from the grave than the male descendants.

In ancient Chinese society, the male had to earn his living and support the family. The female did the housework and looked after the children. In these circumstances, it was preferable that the male descendants should fare better than the female descendants. This concept was known as the *Dao* of the Yin-Yang.

Generally speaking, if either the Green Dragon or White Tiger side was higher than the other, it should not be too high or it would overwhelm members of the other sex.

Then there are many layers of Green Dragons and White Tiger. They are divided into *Internal* and the *Encompassing* Dragons or Tigers respectively.

In the case of this particular grave, the Internal White Tiger is indeed stronger than the Green Dragon.

THE FAIRER SEX BENEFITTED MORE

The result of this formation was that this ancestor grave did actually benefit the female descendants. The ancestor who was buried there was the father. The son eventually became involved in various business but his core activities were in property development and later, in plantations.

Throughout his long and chequered career, he had his fair share of ups and downs. Despite the setbacks, he acquired a reputation for being honest and fair in his business dealings.

When it came to his children, it was the daughters who joined him in the property and plantation company. In fact, one of the daughters is currently running the day to day affairs of the conglomerate. She has been very much in the limelight of the journalists who covered business news for general newspapers and business periodicals.

His sons were also successful in their own right but they did not achieve a similar degree of success compared to the daughters.

Although the fact that the White Tiger side is stronger benefitted the female descendants, it was not enough. There were also other contributory factors.

THE OTHER FACTORS

One such factor was that the White Tiger crossed over the *Ming Tang* or Bright Hall. This feature would give stronger benefits to the female members of the family.

Another important feature in front of this grave is a small little hill that we called the Table Mountain. This Table Mountain had the function of locking auspicious *Qi* so that the wealth luck can be retained. There was also a huge body of water that helps the *Qi* to be retained.

It has often been said that "First is Destiny, second is Luck, third is *feng shui* and fourth is deeds."

Feng Shui came in third because it is believed that *feng shui* can alter one's destiny and in the early days it was achieved through the use of Yin *feng shui*.

Yin *feng shui* depended on the Dragons for its strength. The term Dragons used here in the study of Yin *feng shui* referred to the mountain ranges. This was because Guo Pu in his *"Book of Burial"* mentioned that the Dragons were the beginning source of *Qi*.

How the Dragons came, turned, the shape of the Dragons, how they embraces and how they exited were the focal points in selecting good burial lands. Good or auspicious Dragon *Qi* can bring many benefits to the descendants ranging from wealth, high positions, promotion, nobility and a great line of descendants.

The effects of Yin house *feng shui* or the ancestral grave cannot be ignored. If the layman was ignorant or sceptical of how a good ancestor grave could become beneficial, he would suffer the consequences of a bad ancestral grave due to his ignorance.

It has nothing to do with whether or not one believed or disbelieved in *feng shui*. One did not need to have faith in the medicine before taking it to cure the sickness.

If human existence cannot avoid or overcome Death, then human beings would not escape the ill effects of a bad ancestor grave. Those persons who were in the know and took due care about their ancestors' graves would eventually see the benefits.

CHAPTER SEVEN
LIVE GRAVE 壽墳 OR SHENG JI 生基

In the original practice of *feng shui*, practitioners were hired to design auspicious graves for the deceased. It was only after a period of time had elapsed that the demand arose for practitioners to design or rectify flow of auspicious *Qi* for buildings which housed the living descendants.

Therefore, the concept of preparing a live grave 壽墳 or Sheng Ji 生基 was an ancient practice. However, the very idea of arranging a live grave for the person while he was still alive might outrage the sensibilities of people who came from the Western cultures.

The Chinese believed that each person was born with a fixed destiny. The human being could make some choices during his lifetime; these choices and the timing of the decisions made might affect his Fate.

However, by and large, he would still have to travel along Life's given path, with some minor deviations. Some persons were fated to become famous explorers such as Zheng He, others might become generals or officials of the Imperial court. And at the other end of the human spectrum might be found those persons who were ordinary peasants or even people who had to endure both poverty and sickness.

If everything was preordained, then the question should be asked whether or not we could change our Fate? The destiny could be changed by several ways. One possible way might be to do a lot of good deeds. Another possibility could be by our own effort, although we would have to exert a good deal of effort before we could see any plausible result. The third possibility was to try and alter the destiny energy by manipulating *feng shui Qi* or energy. That was where the concept of live grave came into play.

With the advancements made in physics during the last century, we now know that the tiniest particle of matter is an atom. There are protons, neutrons and electrons that made up the atom. But more to the point, each atom was also a form of energy.

Therefore, it could be said that a human being comprised of a system of atomic arrangements. This caused the *Qi* or energy to flow within that human body. That was the basis on which acupuncture, foot reflexology, *Tai Chi* and *Qigong* worked.

The art of Sheng Ji is very much assimilated from the theory of Yin Feng Shui.

In the study of Yin *Feng Shui*, the practitioner has to use the Earth energy as the major source of *Qi*. In order for earth to sustain plant and animal life, earth must have some energy. To the layman, the earth was used to grow plants and as a place for living things to stand on.

But the *feng shui* practitioner, in common with the archaeologist and the palaeontologist, knew that there were many treasures hidden beneath the earth. The *feng shui* practitioner sought to trace the energy in the earth, then work out ways how to harness this energy so that he could design the live grave 壽坟 for his clients.

The origins of Sheng Ji 生基 have been traced as far back to the Jin dynasty (1115-1234). The *feng shui* master, Guo Pu, wrote in his *Burial Book or Zhang Shu*, that the bones of the ancestors had long lasting effect on the future of their descendants. After all, archaeologists and palaeontologists have found bones that were thousands of years old. The reason why the bones of the ancestors, if buried in an auspicious grave, could benefit the descendants was that the descendants shared the same DNA as the long ago deceased ancestor.

He further postulated that the source of *Qi* can be derived from the mountains and waters when properly captured can benefit their descendants.

> *Earth is the body of Qi, thus having Earth is having Qi while Qi is the source of water.* - *Guo Pu, Zhang Shu*

That was also the same reason why our reader could not possibly benefit from the auspicious grave of another person's ancestor, such as the deceased grandfather of his neighbour! There could be no hitch hiking on the deceased ancestor of someone not related to us.

In order to carry out a Sheng Ji 生基 exercise, we would require some personal effects of the living person. These items could be as simple as the fingernails or the hairs of the person because they contained the DNA of that person.

Since Sheng Ji 生基 was a by-product of doing live grave 壽坟, they shared a common origin in the practice of Daoism. There was a legend of a Daoist monk who built his own live grave 壽坟 which he fancifully called "Tomb of the Living Dead." He was said to have stayed inside that grave for seven years. After he decided to come out of the live grave and return to the world of the living, he had a successful career. This illustrated how the energy of the earth could be harnessed to benefit the *feng shui* living person. Later on, Guo Pu discovered this method and explained it in his writings.

From the era of at least the Song dynasty onwards (960-1279) to the modern nations of China, Taiwan and Hong Kong, many wealthy and prominent families have subscribed to the concept of preparing live graves 壽坟.

The concept of Sheng Ji 生基 is similar to the principles of Yin house *feng shui*. The practitioner kept a wary eye searching for good mountain ranges and their accompanying bodies of water. It was the way water entered, passed through and exited the tombs and where the body of mountain lies that made all the difference between the auspicious tomb and the inauspicious tomb.

In the study of *feng shui*, mountains or dragons affected human relationships and character. The water determined the wealth factors.

CASE STUDY 1: HEALTH IS WEALTH

A female client who was then in her forties had everything to look forward in life. She had played a key role in steering her family business to grow into a flourishing business empire.

So she was devastated to learn from her doctors that she had been diagnosed with the advanced stages of a terminal sickness such as cancer. There was a Chinese saying that "White haired person had to mourn black haired person". This meant that if the parents had to mourn the death of one or more of their children, then the younger generation passed away before the older generation.

She hastily consulted a reputable Sheng Ji 生基 master. To be frank, this person was not yours truly but the *feng shui* master of the writer of this article!

After the Sheng Ji 生基 was completed, she gradually made a recovery from her terminal illness. She has not only resumed her work at her family's business but also participated in many sport activities.

However, perhaps we should not ascribe the credit fully to Sheng Ji 生基. She also played a role by discarding unhealthy bad habits, monitored her medication and implemented a healthy diet lifestyle.

Therefore, Sheng Ji 生基 had to work at two levels. One level was to harness the auspicious *Qi to improve the longevity luck*, the other was to make a personal effort and not become complacent after doing the *feng shui*.

CASE STUDY 2: WHERE IS THE MONEY?

Our next client, Joe, was – well, very much your average Joe. He had been previously working for other people and made creditable progress in his career. After some time, he became discontented and decided to quit to start his own business.

In the first year, he made some money but after that it became a downhill slide. In frustration, he came for a destiny consultation. The reading confirmed that his luck had expired because his luck cycle had changed.

The Chinese have a saying, "When the time has passed, even gold will turn into iron. When the time is right, even iron will turn into gold."

What to do if the person's birth chart did not show any favourable prospects in the immediate future? In that case, we have to turn to *feng shui*, in this case he chose to plant a Sheng Ji 生基, in order to improve the luck prospects.

Since his requirement was for wealth rather than health, I had to select a plot of land that could help remedy his problems. There were two converging rivers that passed through this plot. One of the rivers exited on the left side of the land. The rivers were long and meandering which indicated good wealth and health factors.

Behind the plot of land, there was a mountain range which gave good backing. There were also multiple hills facing the land as well as on the right hand side of the land. These features brought continuous growth and further strengthened the Sheng Ji 生基.

Several months later, Joe was a much happier man. He said that he managed to clinch a few orders. Previously, he was the one who made all the cold calls, now there were people calling him. He was able to meet people who introduced him to other people who could assist him. He found that deals were easier to negotiate and close than before. Well, he is still far from being a millionaire but our average Joe is certainly now a much happier Joe.

What was the difference in the "before" and "after" pictures? It was the difference between perseverance and stubbornness. A person could be stubborn enough to refuse to admit defeat, yet end up as a financial failure. Another person could persevere and make a breakthrough.

If we harnessed the auspicious *Qi* in a competent manner, and if we showed some sincerity and performed good deeds, then our luck would improve with the passage of time.

PART TWO
REFLECTIONS FROM THE EDITOR'S DESK

When this writer first met Alan Chong at an informal function in the early spring of 2013, there was nothing to indicate that the relationship would be anything more than a fleeting acquaintance.

Then, on one late autumn day in 2015, he mentioned that he wanted to write his maiden book about *feng shui*.

That book would attempt to debunk some of the common, popular myths held by the layman about *feng shui*. Instead, it would strive to explain to the same layman a few of the concepts behind authentic, lineage *feng shui*. This knowledge was generally closely held to the chests of lineage *feng shui* masters, most of whom were long deceased. It was only through their texts that some of these well-guarded secrets were gradually revealed.

In other words, Alan showed a marked disdain for the more fashionable New Age *feng shui* which was all agog over lucky charms, good luck symbols, space cleansing and, sometimes even semi-religious practices such as writing auspicious sentences for 49 times. He had even encountered some practitioners who disguised their methods as Classical Feng Shui School but their sources were unclear.

We demurred and listened to his plans with an air of weariness and wariness. After all, we had heard it all before from various people in this industry.

THE EAGER BEAVERS

"Nothing to say, and no idea how to say it"

B.M.W. Young and P.D.R. Gardiner, *"Intelligent Reading"*, 1964

These eager beavers tried to corner you, anxious to tell you all about their plans to write this book or that book. You waited for a few weeks. The weeks quickly turned into months. After several months had passed, they still had not written even a few paragraphs, let alone an entire page, not to mention a single chapter.

By comparison, the female of the species who had become pregnant would have delivered a baby after nine months!

There seemed to be many a slip between the pen and the paper. Why should this proposal be any different?

However, to our disbelief, he did find the time to write and send his first chapter. He wanted to seek some editorial assistance. He also asked for some guidance about finding a reliable and reputable publisher.

So we complied with his requests. There seemed to be no reason to turn down a wannabe, earnest writer – provided he backed his words with his pen.

"THE LION AND THE MOUSE" – AN AESOP'S FABLE

As the material began to trickle in, the structure of the book gradually began to take shape. After some parleying, we agreed that the book should comprise of ten chapters. He should strive to write the lion's share of seven chapters. After all, this was supposed to be his maiden book!

We made a colossal effort to become indolent by contributing a measly three chapters. After all, we reasoned, we had also done some editorial work for the entire book. Why should we write more than the mouse's share of the chapters?

THE MEANING OF TEN

"Numbers are the masters of the weak but the slaves of the strong."

Charles Babbage, *"Passages from the life of a philosopher"*, 1864

But frivolity aside, actually there was a deeper, underlying reason for our request. In the study of *feng shui*, one represented commencement and ten represented completion. Hence, we should offer ten chapters only to our readers. No encores, not one chapter more nor one chapter less.

To return to the concepts of *feng shui*, seven represented fire and three represented wood. In the production cycle, wood produced fire. Therefore, a three to seven ratio of chapters was a supportive relationship.

Initially, it seemed to be basic common sense that both of us should be named as co-authors. However, upon further reflection, we eschewed the role of co-author. Since we did some editorial work, we preferred the moniker of editor.

But we had also contributed some material. So we transposed from being editor to contributing editor.

This might seem a rather academic exercise. By declining to be named as co-author, we think that an analogy might be drawn to the field of aviation.

A FLIGHT OF DIGRESSION: AN ODE TO THE MOSQUITO AND THE DAKOTA

"Those Magnificent Men in Their Flying Machines"

Title of film, 1965
Starring Terry Thomas, Sarah Miles, Stuart Whitman

Instead of becoming co-pilot, we had chosen to become the navigator. If we possessed the fertile imagination of Walter Mitty, it was as though we asked to be transferred from being co-pilot of the Douglas DC-3 Dakota transport aircraft to become the navigator of the De Havilland DH 98 Mosquito bomber.

For the benefit of our readers who were not aviation buffs, perhaps we should offer some brief commentaries about this pair of truly outstanding aircraft.

Both aircraft were twin engined, twin seat types of the Second World War era. The C-47 Skytrain, better known as the DC-3 Dakota was a transport aircraft flown by a pilot and co-pilot. It could carry twenty one fully laden paratroopers.

The Mosquito was a light bomber, constructed entirely from wood so it was known as *"The Wooden Wonder."* Its crew consisted of a pilot and a navigator. There were fighter, bomber, night fighter and photo reconnaissance versions. The Mosquito was so fast that the photo reconnaissance version was unarmed, depending on its high speed to escape. In that sense, it was similar to the DC-3 Dakota which was also unarmed. However, Mosquito missions were generally more hazardous than Dakota sorties.

Therefore, anyone who chose to leave the co-pilot's seat of a Dakota for the navigator's seat of a Mosquito might not expect to survive the war!

Despite being a humble, defenceless transport aircraft, the DC-3 Dakota made such a profound impression on General Dwight Eisenhower that he considered it as one of the four significant weapons of the war.[1]

The demand for these sturdy, versatile aircraft was so great that both the Dakota and the Mosquito remained in service even after jet aircraft had entered service towards the last years of the Second World War.

---

[1] *"Jane's Encyclopaedia of Aviation"*, Crescent Books, 1995, edited Michael Taylor.

The last Mosquito mission flown by the RAF (Royal Air Force) was a photo reconnaissance flight in December 1955, during the Malayan Emergency[2].

The DC-3 Dakota was widely used as a passenger airliner after the war. During the Vietnam War, the Dakota had a fresh lease of life as the AC-47 Gunship, colloquially known as *"Puff the Magic Dragon."* Some crews joked that the "A" in the designation AC-47 stood for "Ancient"[3]!

They might not know it at that time but Arthur E Raymond[4] and Geoffrey de Havilland (later Sir Geoffrey) were the magnificent men who designed in December 1935 and October 1938 respectively what would eventually become the legendary Dakota and Mosquito.

CONCLUSION

The fact that the manuscript was completed and the end result was a book that reached the hands of the reader was testimony to the grit and determination of Alan Chong. It was an incredible achievement, given that most aspiring writers do not translate their intentions into actions.

Throughout this book, we have preferred to use the more informal, editorial "we" rather than the more personal pronoun "I".

---

[2] *"Wings of Fame"*, Volume 18, Aerospace Publications, 2000. The article on the Mosquito was contributed by Martin Bowman. It was titled *"de Havilland DH. 98 Mosquito (Bomber and PR variants) Part I"*. Sadly, *Part II* was never published. *"Wings of Fame"* ceased publication after Volume 20.

[3] *"Combat Aircraft of World War II"*, Tiger Books, 2000. This out of print gem was profusely illustrated in colour, with many cutaway drawings, by Bill Gunston.

[4] Ibid, *"Combat Aircraft of World War II"*, Bill Gunston

ACKNOWLEDGMENTS

This book would not have been possible without the material assistance of our publishers. In particular, we would like to thank Angel Chavez for urging us to finish the manuscript and Sydney Felicio for her infinite patience by periodically asking us whether the manuscript was ready.

INTRODUCTION TO BA ZI

For the benefit of our readers who may not be familiar with *Ba Zi*, we have written a brief technical introduction to the subject.

The fundamental basis in the study of *Ba Zi* was the five elements. These elements are 木 wood, 火 fire, 土 earth, 金 metal and 水 water.

These five elements had relationships with each other in three cycles. The first of these cycles was the production cycle, followed by the weakening cycle and the controlling cycle.

THE PRODUCTION CYCLE

In the production cycle, the wood produced the fire. For instance, the wood provided the fuel to burn the fire.

After the fire had burnt up the wood, the wood was said to be turned into ashes. Therefore, the fire produced the earth.

The earth was considered to produce the metal because the metal was buried inside the earth. In order to extract the metal, we had to dig or bore into the earth to expose the metal.

The metal produced water because the metal could be forged by fire until the metal rod melted. When the metal rod melted, the metal was said to have liquefied.

Perhaps it would be easier to understand the concepts if we presented the cycles in the form of diagrams.

Table 1: The Production Cycle

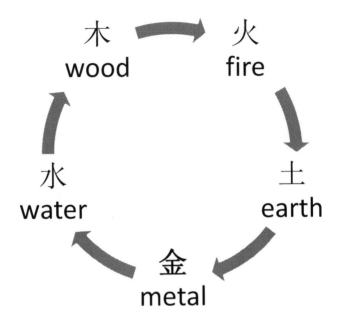

THE CONTROLLING CYCLE

In the controlling cycle, wood was said to control earth. For instance, the roots of the tree gripped the soil. Earth was deemed to control water such as when the banks of the river prevented the water from overflowing. The water was considered to control the fire by putting out the fire. The fire controlled the metal by melting the metal and forging it.

The controlling cycle was the production cycle in reverse.

Table 2: The Controlling Cycle

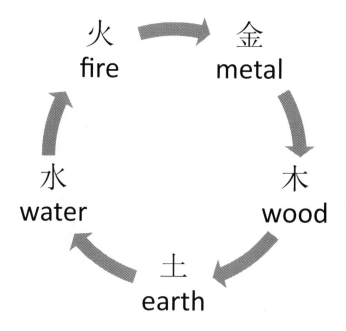

THE WEAKENING CYCLE

In the weakening cycle, the wood weakened the water. The tree obtained nourishment from the water inside the earth. In this way, the wood reduced the water available in the earth.

The water weakened the metal. Alternately, the presence of water could also be said to rust the metal.

The metal weakened the earth. When the earth produced too many minerals or too much metal, the earth became depleted.

The earth weakened the fire by causing the fire to become dim. When firemen tried to put out a fire, they usually made use of water. In the event that water was not available or was insufficient, they could resort to pouring some earth onto the fire. However, if the fire was too strong or spreading too fast, earth alone would not be sufficient to douse the fire.

The weakening cycle could be considered to come in between the production cycle and the controlling cycle.

Table 3: The Weakening Cycle

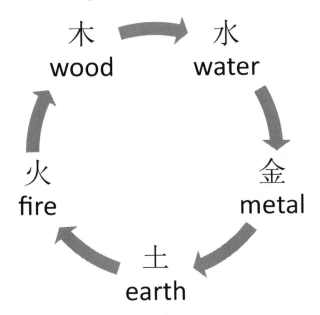

There are also ten Heavenly Stems, commencing with 甲 Jia wood and ending with 癸 Gui water. The Heavenly Stems are usually arranged in accordance with the production cycle. They are called Heavenly Stems because they appear at the top of the *Ba Zi* chart.

Table 4: The Ten Heavenly Stems

甲	乙	丙	丁	戊	己	庚	辛	壬	癸
Jia	*Yi*	*Bing*	*Ding*	*Wu*	*Ji*	*Geng*	*Xin*	*Ren*	*Gui*
Wood	Wood	Fire	Fire	Earth	Earth	Metal	Metal	Water	Water

Then there are the twelve Earthly Branches. To the layman, these may also be colloquially known as the twelve animals.

Table 5: The Twelve Earthly Branches

子	丑	寅	卯	辰	巳	午	未	申	酉	戌	亥
Zi	*Chou*	*Yin*	*Mao*	*Chen*	*Si*	*Wu*	*Wei*	*Shen*	*You*	*Xu*	*Hai*
Rat	Ox	Tiger	Rabbit	Dragon	Snake	Horse	Goat	Monkey	Rooster	Dog	Pig

Let us stop our explanations at this juncture. We had to seek a balance between giving a brief introduction and going into too much technical detail. If we did not offer some sort of introduction, the layman reader might be lost. If we provided too much of the technical stuff, that same reader might be lost.

CHAPTER EIGHT
IN THE BEGINNING, THERE WAS MONEY

Since money was almost everybody's favourite topic, let discuss money in our first *Ba Zi* article.

WHO WANTS TO READ A *BA ZI* CHART?

This was the birth chart of a male person who became a multi-millionaire in real estate. In order to preserve his anonymity, we shall not reveal his identity. To be more precise, he made his money in property development such as construction of a shopping mall, an exhibition and conference centre, a theme park and hotel.

Male Millionaire 19 August 1955

时Hour	日Day	月Month			年Year		
辛 Xin Metal	壬 Ren Water	甲 Jia Wood			乙 Yi Wood		
亥 Hai Pig	子 Zi Rat	申 Shen Monkey			未 Wei Goat		
壬 Ren Water	甲 Jia Wood	癸 Gui Water	庚 Geng Metal	壬 Ren Water	戊 Wu Earth	己 Ji Earth	丁 Ding Fire	乙 Yi Wood

When we read a birth chart, we needed a starting point or a point of reference. The starting point was the person's day of birth.

When we mentioned the day of birth, we did not mean that he was born on the 19th of the month or even whether he was born on Monday or Tuesday. Instead, we meant the Chinese character shown on the top box of his day pillar.

In this case, that Chinese character was 壬 Ren water. Therefore, we say that he was a 壬 Ren water day master. Every other element in the chart had to be referenced back to this day master.

WHERE IS THE MONEY?

Money, money, money

Music & Lyrics by Benny Andersson & Bjorn Ulvaues

Mon-ey, mon-ey mon-ey   must be fun-ny   in a richman's world

Since this was the chart of a male person, the main concern was money because the male was supposed to support his family.

In the controlling cycle, water is said to control fire. The fire element was the wealth to the water person.

One elementary way to ascertain whether he had wealth might be to look for the fire element in his chart. In this chart, there was only one fire element. It was the 丁 Ding fire which was found inside his 未 Goat year.

THE UNCERTAIN HOUR

In an effort to be frank, we must categorically state here that this person's hour of birth was not known with certainty. We have deduced his hour of birth based on events in his life, his family relationships and his character.

He was known to be fair and honest in his business dealings. He had good relationships with his children, especially his daughters.

In fact, one daughter eventually became his successor in his flagship company. Since this person was already elderly, there were sufficient events that occurred late in his life which provided further clues to deducing his birth hour. We believed that we have worked out his birth hour within a reasonable degree of accuracy.

If the hour of birth was correct, then there was no fire in the hour pillar. In that case, it left us with only one fire element in his birth chart.

HOW DO WE KNOW WHO IS RICH AND WHO IS POOR?

The next question that we should ask ourselves was, if a person had only one wealth element in his chart, did that indicate he was wealthy or poor?

There was at least one well-known school of *Phat Chee* which taught that the more wealth stars there were in the birth chart, the wealthier was the person.

This line of thinking was mistaken. Instead of the more wealth stars the merrier, the truly wealthy person has only a few wealth stars.

Although the presence of the wealth stars was a simple way to deduce whether there was wealth in the chart, we were also curious to know when the wealth would arrive and how long it would last.

WHY SHOULD WE ANALYSE THE STRUCTURE OF THE CHART?

Let us probe deeper by analyzing the structure of the chart. If we looked at the bottom half of the birth chart, we found that he was born on a 子 Rat day, in the 申 Monkey month and probably during the 亥 Pig hour.

The 申 Monkey month indicated that he was born in the autumn season. The strongest *Qi* or energy during autumn was metal. In the production cycle, metal produced water. Therefore, his 壬 Ren water day master was considered strong.

On one side of the chart, his 子 Rat day had a Three Harmony Combination[5] with his 申 Monkey month to produce water.

On the other side of the chart, his 子 Rat day had a Seasonal Combination[6] with his 亥 Pig hour that also resulted in water.

These combinations could be illustrated as follows:-

子 Rat (day) + 申 Monkey (month) = 水 water

子 Rat (day) + 亥 Pig (hour) = 水 water

The result of all these combinations meant that his 壬 water day master, which was already strong, had become overly strong.

THE ONE THING NEEDED

In order to rectify the situation, the presence of earth, especially 戊 Wu earth, was needed. In the controlling cycle, earth was deemed to control water. But this earth had to be the 戊 Wu earth which represented the hard rocks of the mountains.

If there was only 己 Ji earth, it would not be able to control the strong water. The 己 Ji earth represented the soft muddy earth of clay and mud. It could absorb water and was useful for growing crops. But it was too soft and porous to control the raging waters.

HOW CAN A PERSON BECOME WEALTHY WITHOUT ANY WEALTH STARS?

This person started his property development company in 1984 which was the year of 甲子 Wood Rat. Four years later, in 1988, he

---

[5] *Three Harmony Combination comprised of* 申 *SHEN* + 子 *ZI* + 辰 *CHEN.*
[6] *Seasonal Combination of water comprised of* 亥 *HAI* + 子 *ZI* + 丑 *CHOU*

struck gold when the year of 戊辰 Earth Dragon arrived. He was then aged 34 and about to commence his luck cycle of 庚辰 Metal Dragon.

Male Millionaire Early Luck Cycle

34	24	14	4
庚 Geng Metal	辛 Xin Metal	壬 Ren Water	癸 Gui Water
辰 Chen Dragon	巳 Si Snake	午 Wu Horse	未 Wei Goat
戊 乙 癸 Wu Yi Gui Earth Wood Water	丙 戊 庚 Bing Wu Geng Fire Earth Metal	丁 已 Ding Ji Fire Earth	已 丁 乙 Ji Ding Yi Earth Fire Wood

Since he was a 壬 Ren water person, his wealth element should have been fire. There was no fire in the luck cycle of 庚辰 Metal Dragon or the annual pillar of 戊辰 Earth Dragon.

Some people argued that if a person were to become rich, he should have many wealth stars in his birth chart. In that case, how did they propose to explain why these two birth charts had no wealth stars, yet the persons concerned became rich and famous?

Furthermore, why did he have to wait for the arrival of another 辰 Dragon before he struck gold?

"ENTER THE DRAGON"

When 戊 Wu earth was found in the 辰 Dragon and the 戌 Dog, it was considered thick and heavy earth. He had one 辰 Dragon in his luck cycle of 庚辰 Metal Dragon. In 1988, another Dragon arrived in the form of the 戊辰 Earth Dragon year. The presence of the two 辰 Dragons meant that he had plenty of thick and heavy 戊 Wu earth.

It was this thick and heavy 戊 Wu earth that brought him the luck. It did not matter one iota if there was no fire (which was his wealth element) in the two 辰 Dragons. When his luck came in the two 辰 Dragons, the wealth would come even though the fire element was not available.

In fact, his luck was so strong during this period that his company was not seriously affected by the financial crisis in 1987. During the decade of his 庚辰 Metal Dragon luck cycle from the age of 34 to 43, his company expanded by leaps and bounds. From 1994 to 1997, his company enjoyed bountiful years.

ALL THINGS CHANGE IN THE UNIVERSE

However, from the age of 44, he entered his luck cycle of 己卯 Earth Rabbit. The 戊 Wu earth that he needed was no longer available. This change of luck cycle was the harbinger of his future troubles.

Male Millionaire Late Luck Cycle (continued)

74	64		54			44
丙 Bing Fire	丁 Ding Fire		戊 Wu Earth			己 Ji Earth
子 Zi Rat	丑 Chou Ox		寅 Yin Tiger			卯 Mao Rabbit
癸 Gui Water	己 Ji Earth	癸 Gui Water	辛 Xin Metal	甲 Jia Wood	丙 Bing Fire	戊 Wu Earth	乙 Yi Wood

He commenced the luck cycle of 己卯 Earth Rabbit in the year 1998. The Asian financial crisis broke out in 1997. This time round, he would not be able to escape the fallout from this Asian financial crisis.

As if it was not bad enough that there was financial contagion in the Asian region, there was also a political crisis in Malaysia. The Prime Minister at that time, Dr Mahathir Mohamad sacked his Deputy Prime Minister, Anwar Ibrahim. Therefore, there were two parallel crises occurring at the same time.

"TIGER, TIGER BURNING BRIGHT"

"Tiger, Tiger, burning bright,
In the forests of the night,
What immortal hand or eye
Could frame thy fearful symmetry?"

William Blake,
"Songs of Experience", 1794

His next luck cycle was the 戊寅 Earth Tiger luck cycle from the age of 54. The presence of the 戊 Wu Earth should have brought him some relief.

But his fortunes did not markedly improve from 2009. This was the first year of his new luck cycle. The reason was that the 戊 Wu Earth was not thick and heavy in the 寅 Tiger. Instead, the main *Qi* in the 寅 Tiger was the 甲 Jia wood. This 甲 Jia wood controlled the 戊 Wu Earth. The 甲 Jia wood Heavenly Stem could be said to be obstructing the 戊 Wu Earth.

The other factor was that the 寅 Tiger luck cycle clashed with his 申 Monkey month. He was a 壬 Ren water day master. The 申 Monkey month was vital to him because the 申 Monkey was the source of Heavenly Water.

In the Chinese classics, it has been written that when 壬 Ren water was found in the 申 Monkey, the headstream of the waters would be far and long. Therefore, when the 申 Monkey was afflicted by a clash or punishment, it would be detrimental to the 壬 Ren water.

WHAT MIGHT HAPPEN WHEN TWO 亥 PIGS MEET?

In the year 2007, this person sold some of the most valuable properties among his assets. With the money raised from this disposal, the business minded entrepreneur began to search for avenues to invest his gains.

He purchased about 2,000 acres of land from another financially distressed property developer at reportedly bargain prices. However, it remained to be seen whether or not his company would be able to make a handsome profit from the development of this vast acreage in the future.

In the same year of 2007, he also bought some oil palm plantation land. His company then offered a profit sharing scheme to the public. The interested investor would pay some money in return for some share of the profits from the harvest and sale of the palm oil.

The investor would be given shares ranging from about one quarter of an acre to one acre of oil palm land. The amount of returns that the investor could expect varied in proportion to the size of his investment.

In order to attract potential investors, the company guaranteed to pay a minimum amount as dividends. But the fluctuations in the price of palm oil meant that sometimes there were shortfalls between the profits and the promised dividends. The company had to make good the difference since they had guaranteed the minimum returns. In 2013, the company decided to cut their losses and terminate this scheme by paying back the investors.

This person had a moral and upright character. His company kept their word, refunded the investors and aborted the ill-fated scheme.

If we traced back the origins of this problem, then it could arguably be said that it commenced in 2007 with the venture into another business, oil palm plantation.

The year 2007 was the year of 丁亥 Fire Pig. This 亥 Pig year had a self-punishment relationship with his 亥 Pig hour of birth. This could be interpreted to mean that he might do something that would bring problems.

From 2009, he commenced his luck cycle of 戊寅 Earth Tiger. The 寅 Tiger had a combination with his 亥 Pig hour of birth that resulted in wood. This wood represented his productivity or output. Therefore, there was some possibility that he might be able to dispose of some of his assets.

"BACK TO THE FUTURE"

At the time of writing, this person made a corporate announcement that he was ready to make a comeback. Will he be able to return to the glory days when the share price of his company soared to dizzying heights?

The year 2018 would be the year of the 戊戌 Earth Dog. Since the 戊 Wu Earth was thick and heavy during the 戌 Dog year, he would have an excellent year in 2018. However, that good fortune would last only one year.

The 丑 Ox had a combination with his 子 Rat day of birth that resulted in earth. The presence of this earth would assist him in his recovery. But his return to the corporate world would probably not be as successful as before, compared to the golden era of his two 辰 Dragons.

He might be wealthy and successful but his company did not make it to the top ten in a list of best property developers drawn up by a local business weekly. For that matter, he was also not listed in the top 40 wealthiest Malaysians in a bi-weekly local business magazine.

But did these rankings really matter? Perhaps it mattered more to those who yearned to be included in the A lists. What was far more important than any rankings, local or global, was that this wealthy person had a moral and upright character. That was something that all the money in the world could not buy.

After all, *"Character is Destiny."*

CHAPTER NINE
PLAYING WITH FIRE: THE SPECIAL CASE OF "THE FIRE HOUR"

What was meant by the term "day master?"

In the study of Ba Zi, there are ten Heavenly Stems. These Heavenly Stems began with wood and follow the production cycle until it ended in water. There is a Heavenly Stem for each day of the year. After the cycle of ten Heavenly Stems is completed, the cycle would repeat itself. Therefore, on any given day of birth, the person would have a Heavenly Stem shown on his day pillar of birth. This Heavenly Stem on the date of birth is known as the "day master."

To recap, the table of the ten Heavenly Stems has been shown again:-

Table 5: The Ten Heavenly Stems

甲 Jia Wood	乙 Yi Wood	丙 Bing Fire	丁 Ding Fire	戊 Wu Earth
己 Ji Earth	庚 Geng Metal	辛 Xin Metal	壬 Ren Water	癸 Gui Water

The element shown at the top of the day pillar was technically known as the day master. Any element shown at the top of the eight characters (*Ba Zi*) was called the Heavenly Stem. Those elements that appeared at the bottom of the chart were described as the Earthly Branches. To the beginner they could be represented by as the twelve animals.

For instance, the first day of 2016 in the Chinese solar calendar fell on 4 February. If we looked up the Chinese almanac, 4 February 2016 was a 丙辰 Bing Chen (Fire Dragon) day. Therefore, a baby born on this day was said to have a 丙 Bing Fire day master.

According to the tables, the next day after a 丙 Bing Fire was 丁 Ding Fire. The next Earthly Branch after 辰 Chen (Dragon) is 巳 Si (Snake). So another baby born on 5 February 2016 would have been born on a 丁巳 Ding Si (Fire Snake) day. He was said to be a 丁 Ding Fire day master.

Why should the 丙 Bing fire day master be born during the daytime hours?

There was one well-known school of *Ba Zi* which taught that a 丙 Bing Fire day master should be born during the daylight hours.

They argued that the 丙 Bing Fire represented the fire of the sun. The sun shone the brightest during the hours of the day. If the person was born during the hours of the night, the sun had already set. Since the sun could not be seen at night, it implied that if a 丙 Bing Fire day master was born at night, his efforts would not be appreciated.

Why should the 丁 Ding fire day master be born during the hours of the night?

Conversely, if a person was, he had to be born during the night time. The 丁 Ding fire represented the fire of the candle or the stove.

It was during the hours of darkness at night that the 丁 Ding fire of the candle would be most needed. During the daytime, the 丙 Bing Fire of the sun was so bright that the 丁 Ding fire was not required.

With the coming of dawn, people would put out the 丁 Ding fire of the candle.

The inference was that the 丁 Ding fire day master had to be born at night in order to have any achievements in life.

In short, woe betide the 丙 Bing Fire or 丁 Ding fire day master who had the misfortune to be born during the wrong hours. They would definitely not become successful during their life time. The fire day master was considered as a "special case" because they had to be born during the "right" hours.

These arguments seemed sound and rational, solidly backed by logical reasoning. Before we proceed further, let us offer a brief explanation of how the Chinese derived their hours of birth. It was quite different from Western astrology.

What was the Chinese concept of time?

In the study of *Ba Zi*, there were twelve Earthly Branches and twenty four hours in one day. Therefore, each Earthly Branch had to cover a time span of two hours.

The following table showed a simplified version of each of the twelve Earthly Branches and the hours that they represented.

Table 6: Simplified Table of the Hours of Birth

Hour of birth	Earthly Branch
11 pm to 11.59 am	Late 子 Rat hour
12 am to 12.59 am	Early 子 Rat hour
1 am to 2.59 am	丑 Ox hour
3 am to 4.59 am	寅 Tiger hour
5 am to 6.59 am	卯 Rabbit hour
7 am to 8.59 am	辰 Dragon hour

9 am to 10.59 am	巳 Snake hour
11 am to 12.59 pm	午 Horse hour
1 pm to 2.59 pm	未 Goat hour
3 pm to 4.59 pm	申 Monkey hour
5 pm to 6.59 pm	酉 Rooster hour
7 pm to 8.59 pm	戌 Dog hour
9 pm to 10.59 pm	亥 Pig hour

Some schools of *Ba Zi* defined the two hour zones from, say, 1 am to 2.59 am. However, there were also other *Ba Zi* schools which listed the two hours as 1 am to 3 am and the next two hours as 3.01 am to 5 am.

This was only a simplified version of the actual table showing the hours of birth. The full table of the hours should show the Heavenly Stems of the birth hours as well.

However, as this article was meant for the beginner who presumably was not familiar with the study of *Ba Zi*, we do not propose to explain in greater detail how to derive the Heavenly Stems for the hours of birth.

Was the theory of the special hour of birth for fire day masters really valid? In order to find out, let us put the theory to the simple litmus test by briefly examining a potpourri of the charts of fire day masters.

PART ONE: THE 丙 BING FIRE DAY MASTER

Steve Jobs needed no introduction to our readers. Even after his death, the influence of his work and his company's products were felt throughout most of the connected world.

Steve Jobs 24 February 1955

时Hour			日Day			月Month			年Year		
戊			丙			戊			乙		
Wu			Bing			Wu			Yi		
Earth			Fire			Earth			Wood		
戌			辰			寅			未		
Xu			Chen			Yin			Wei		
Dog			Dragon			Tiger			Goat		
戊	辛	丁	戊	乙	癸	甲	丙	戊	己	丁	乙
Wu	Xin	Ding	Wu	Yi	Gui	Jia	Bing	Wu	Ji	Ding	Yi
Earth	Metal	Fire	Earth	Wood	Water	Wood	Fire	Earth	Earth	Fire	Wood

But there was only one flaw. Steve Jobs was a 丙 Bing fire day master who had the "misfortune" to be born at night. He was born at 7.15 pm, after the sun had set.

💣 If the theory of the fire hour was valid, how could the proponents of this theory explain why a 丙 Bing fire day master born at night could become wealthy and famous?

Every four years, thousands of football fans throughout the world congregate around their TV screens to watch the World Cup. Perhaps it was fitting that the first two charts we selected were from the world of football.

The names of Thierry Henry and Patrick Vieira should not need any introduction to most of our readers. These persons have been so frequently mentioned in the sports news that it was safe to say even non-football fans have heard of them.

Here are the charts of Thierry Henry and Patrick Vieira.

Thierry Henry 17 August 1977

时Hour	日Day		月Month			年Year		
丁 Ding Fire	丙 Bing Fire		戊 Wu Earth			丁 Ding Fire		
酉 You Rooster	午 Wu Horse		申 Shen Monkey			巳 Si Snake		
辛 Xin Metal	丁 Ding Fire	已 Ji Earth	庚 Geng Metal	壬 Ren Water	戊 Wu Earth	丙 Bing Fire	戊 Wu Earth	庚 Geng Metal

Patrick Vieira 23 June 1976

时Hour	日Day		月Month			年Year		
庚 Geng Metal	丙 Bing Fire		甲 Jia Wood			丙 Bing Fire		
子 Zi Rat	午 Wu Horse		午 Wu Horse			辰 Chen Dragon		
癸 Gui Water	丁 Ding Fire	已 Ji Earth	丁 Ding Fire	已 Ji Earth	戊 Wu Earth	乙 Yi Water	癸 Gui Wood	

As we could evidently see from the charts, both Thierry Henry and Patrick Vieira were 丙 Bing fire day masters.

💣 What was not so apparent was the fact that both of them were born at night. Thierry Henry was born at 6.45 pm while Patrick Vieira was born even later, at 11.05 pm. How was it possible that two 丙 Bing fire day masters born after sunset could become top professional footballers?

There were some schools of *Ba Zi* which changed the day master after 11 pm to the day master of the next day. What might be the possible unintended consequences of this line of argument or interpretation?

Some schools of *Ba Zi* interpreted that the 丙 Bing fire day master had changed to 丁 Ding fire day master because the day had changed from 11 pm to the next day. The Chinese considered that the midnight hour commenced from 11 pm, not 12 am.

It was up to the individual to decide whether or not they wanted to follow this interpretation. After all, one day had to end and change to the next day. It was only a question of which hour should the changeover take place.

However, if the next day was chosen, it meant that the day master had changed. When we changed the day master, we had also changed the reading of the Ten Gods, the Useful Gods, the Noble Elements and the family members.

The reading of the luck cycles had also changed. Instead of interpreting that a certain luck cycle was favourable, now we might interpret that the same luck cycle was disadvantageous.

On the lighter side, let us look at the chart of a famous female model who tried to be an actress.

Pamela Anderson 1 July 1967

时Hour			日Day			月Month		年Year		
庚 Geng Metal			丙 Bing Fire			丙 Bing Fire		丁 Ding Fire		
寅 Yin Tiger			寅 Yin Tiger			午 Wu Horse		未 Wei Goat		
甲 Jia Wood	丙 Bing Fire	戊 Wu Earth	甲 Jia Wood	丙 Bing Fire	戊 Wu Earth	丁 Ding Fire	己 Ji Earth	己 Ji Earth	丁 Ding Fire	乙 Yi Wood

Pamela Anderson was more famous for revealing her shapely body in the TV series, *"Baywatch"* rather than for any real acting abilities. She had an abusive marriage with Kid Rock.

She was born at 4.08 am, the "wrong" hour of birth for a 丙 Bing fire day master. This quartet of 丙 Bing fire day masters were born after the sun had set. How did proponents of the theory of the fire hour explain why they could become famous and wealthy?

PART TWO: THE 丁 DING FIRE DAY MASTER

In the 1960s, many eminent Americans became involved in movements against escalating US involvement in the Vietnam War. One of these was the singer and songwriter, Joan Baez.

She took part in the inaugural Woodstock festival in 1969. She was also known for her enduring relationship that vacillated between "on" and "off" with Bob Dylan. Her signature song, *"Diamonds and Rust"*, waxed nostalgic about their relationship.

Joan Baez 9 January 1941

时 Hour	日 Day	月 Month	年 Year
乙 Yi Wood	丁 Ding Fire	己 Ji Earth	庚 Geng Metal
巳 Si Snake	巳 Si Snake	丑 Chou Ox	辰 Chen Dragon
丙 戊 庚 Bing Wu Geng Fire Earth Metal	丙 戊 庚 Bing Wu Geng Fire Earth Metal	己 癸 辛 Ji Gui Xin Earth Water Metal	戊 乙 癸 Wu Yi Gui Earth Wood Water

There was only one "flaw". Joan Baez was born at 10.45 am, the hours of daylight which were deemed unsuitable for a 丁 Ding fire day master to have any achievements.

Let us look at the chart of another lady who could not only act but also sing. Glenn Close was known to have performed as a soprano.

Glenn Close 19 March 1947

时Hour			日Day	月Month	年Year	
	丁 Ding Fire		丁 Ding Fire	癸 Gui Water	丁 Ding Fire	
	未 Wei Goat		酉 You Rooster	卯 Mao Rabbit	亥 Hai Pig	
己 Ji Earth	丁 Ding Fire	乙 Yi Wood	辛 Xin Metal	乙 Yi Wood	壬 Ren Water	甲 Jia Wood

Glenn Close was born in a wealthy family. Her father was a Harvard trained surgeon. The family owned a 500 acre estate.

The film director, George Roy Hill had established his reputation by making *"Butch Cassidy and the Sundance Kid"* and *"The Sting"* in 1969 and 1973 respectively. The chemistry between Robert Redford and Paul Newman was a key factor behind the success of these two films.

In 1982, George Roy Hill spotted Glenn Close in the Broadway musical *"Barnum."* He decided to cast her in *"The World according to Garp."* After that, the world of Glenn Close would never be the same again. She had got her break into stardom.

She was nominated for Oscars for her roles in *"The World according to Garp"*, *"The Big Chill"* and *"The Natural."* She also gave memorable performances in *"Fatal Attractions"* and *"Dangerous Liaisons."*

However, there was one "drawback". She was born at 2.12 pm, when the sun was still shining brightly in the sky. Her 丁 Ding fire day master could neither be seen nor appreciated.

Let us look at the chart of a male 丁 Ding fire day master who had the bad luck to be born during the daytime.

Dustin Hoffman 8 August 1937

时Hour	日Day	月Month			年Year		
已 Ji Earth	丁 Ding Fire	戊 Wu Earth			丁 Ding Fire		
酉 You Rooster	卯 Mao Rabbit	申 Shen Monkey			丑 Chou Ox		
辛 Xin Metal	乙 Yi Wood	庚 Geng Metal	壬 Ren Water	戊 Wu Earth	已 Ji Earth	癸 Gui Water	辛 Xin Metal

In 1963, Dustin Hoffman got his break when he was cast as Ben Braddock in *"The Graduate."* He was fresh out of college, looking for a job, inexperienced in work, love and sex. In short, he was ripe for seduction by Mrs Robinson (played by Anne Bancroft).

He gave his arguably most brilliant performance in *"Midnight Cowboy."* He was the crafty Ratso, who accidentally became the mentor of sorts to Joe Buck (Jon Voight), an ambitious but naïve hustler who had just arrived in New York. Ratso had to face crushing poverty and struggle with rapidly declining health issues until he expired towards the end of the movie.

In real life, he also had the "misfortune" to be born during the daytime, at 5.07 pm, before the sun had set.

We began our discussion of the fire hour with the example of someone from the corporate world, Steve Jobs.

Perhaps it might be fitting to close our discussion of the fire hour by returning to the corporate circles. Let us look at the chart of someone from another industry other than computers and animation. We have chosen the chart of Lee Iacocca who made his reputation in the automobiles industry.

Lee Iacocca 15 October 1924

时Hour	日Day	月Month			年Year
己 Ji Earth	丁 Ding Fire	甲 Jia Wood			甲 Jia Wood
酉 You Rooster	卯 Mao Rabbit	戌 Xu Dog			子 Zi Rat
辛 Xin Metal	乙 Yi Wood	戊 Wu Earth	辛 Xin Metal	丁 Ding Fire	癸 Gui Water

Lee Iacocca worked for the Ford Motor Company for 32 years, the last eight years as president of the company. However, his high post brought him into conflict with Henry Ford II. As Ford was the son of the founder of the company, he could not be fired.

Instead, it was Lee Iacocca who was dismissed in July 1978. By then, he was held in such high esteem as a senior manager that offers of employment poured in. However, he wanted to get his own back on Henry Ford II. In order to do that, he had to remain in the automobile industry.

So when the ailing Chrysler Motor Corporation asked him to take over and try to steer the company back to financial health, he readily accepted. By 1983, the company declared its first profit of $925 million.

But Lee Iacocca had the "bad" luck to be born at 5.00 pm, before the sun had set. How could a 丁 Ding fire day master born during the day time ever manage to hold such high position in two corporations?

PART THREE: COMPARISON OF TWO 丁 DING FIRE DAY MASTERS

To recap, according to the theory, a 丁 Ding fire person had to be born at night so that the fire of the candle would shine brightly during the hours of darkness. Then he would have the best chances of success in life.

But if it could be shown that a 丁 Ding fire person born at night was less successful than another 丁 Ding fire person born during the daytime, then perhaps some doubt might be cast on the validity of this theory.

Bruce Boxleitner 12 May 1950

时Hour	日Day	月Month	年Year
壬 Ren Water	丁 Ding Fire	辛 Xin Metal	庚 Geng Metal
寅 Yin Tiger	未 Wei Goat	巳 Si Snake	寅 Yin Tiger
甲 丙 戊 Jia Bing Wu Wood Fire	己 丁 乙 Ji Ding Yi Earth Fire Wood	丙 戊 庚 Bing Wu Geng Fire Earth Metal	甲 丙 戊 Jia Bing Wu Wood Fire Earth

Bruce Boxleitner was a 丁 Ding fire person born 4.40 am. So his birth hour should have assisted him.

Instead, he only enjoyed limited success. He was given a leading role beside James Arness in the made for TV series, *"How the West was won"* (1976 - 1979). Probably the best of the twenty five episodes were *"The Gunfighter"* (Season 3, Episode 1) where he was opposed by, then assisted by the gunfighter, Frank Grayson (Jared Martin) and *"Luke"* (Season 3, Episode 9).

In this series, he gave a convincing portrayal as the gunfighter Luke Machan, one of the second generation of Machans to settle in the West. All the women he was involved with had a melancholic habit of ending up getting killed, such as his Mormon lover, Erika Hanks (Brit Lind) who was hit by a stray bullet while taking shelter behind a log. In the episode *"Luke"*, his lover, Florrie (Belinda Montgomery) stopped a bullet meant for him. His only lover who survived was Hillary (Elyssa Davalos) but surprisingly, the script did not provide for her to marry him.

There was also a movie with the same title, *"How the West was won"*, made earlier, in 1963, and completed by three directors, namely Henry Hathaway, George Marshall and John Ford. To avoid confusion with this movie version, the TV series was sometimes known by the alternative title, *"The Macahans."*

Bruce Boxleitner appeared in many other films but he was chiefly remembered for his part in another TV series, *"Babylon 5."* This series paled in comparison with its more commercially successful rivals – *"Star Trek"* and *"Star Wars."*

In the genre of the Western, there were other actors who surpassed Bruce Boxleitner. Like any other TV series, the producers of *"How the West was won"* had to find ways to attract audiences, especially in the early episodes. So fans of this series were elated to see appearances by Anthony Zerbe and Jack Elam in the first three episodes. Both of them were well established stalwarts of the Western genre.

It was James Arness who was given the top billing as the elderly Zeb Macahan in the TV series, *"How the West was won."* After all, he had cemented his reputation as Marshall Matt Dillon in the longest running TV series, *"Gunsmoke"* (1955 - 1975, 635 episodes in 7 seasons).

Marshall Matt Dillon had a cheerful, harmless deputy, Chester (Dennis Weaver) who did not even wear a gun belt, let alone tote a six shooter! The character of Chester was probably meant to be soft, such as that of an innocent farm hand. Then his character would juxtapose well with the tough profile of Marshall Dillon. The other stalwarts of the long running series were the saloon keeper, Kitty (Amanda Blake) and Doc (Milburn Stone).

To the delight of his fans, James Arness went on to make another five full length *"Gunsmoke"* movies. In the film, *"Gunsmoke: Return to Dodge"* (1987), the producers dedicated it to the memory of two persons, one of whom was Milburn Stone.

In the genre of science fiction, Bruce Boxleitner was outclassed by Harrison Ford and William Shatner in *"Star Wars"* and *"Star Trek"* respectively.

In addition to the TV series, *"Star Trek"*, there were also three full length *"Star Trek"* movies. Although Harrison Ford appeared in only the first trilogy of *"Star Wars"* films, the *"Star Wars"* series eventually expanded to six movies.

Tom Hanks 9 July 1956

时Hour	日Day	月Month	年Year
丙 Bing Fire	丁 Ding Fire	乙 Yi Wood	丙 Bing Fire
午 Wu Horse	丑 Chou Ox	未 Wei Goat	申 Shen Monkey
丁 己 Ding Ji Fire Earth	己 癸 辛 Ji Gui Xin Earth Water Metal	己 丁 乙 Ji Ding Yi Earth Fire Wood	庚 壬 戊 Geng Ren Wu Metal Water Earth

Tom Hanks had memorable roles in *"Saving Private Ryan"* and *"The Polar Express."* In 1994, he was unsurpassable as the moronic, handicapped *"Forrest Gump."* In this film, he had a low IQ of only 75 and was handicapped by a lame leg.

Forrest Gump Theme

Alan Silverstri

Eventually, he made an immense effort to overcome his disability. But he would find that it was not so easy to woo and win over his childhood friend, Jenny Curran. Hanna Hall played Jenny Curran as a child while Robin Wright was the adult size Jenny Curran. Both of them gave commendable performances in their supporting roles.

If we were to search from the older generation of actors who acted in similar genres of the dense dimwit, probably it was James Stewart who was versatile enough to deliver an outstanding performance. He was superb as the elderly, slightly insane Elwood P Dowd in *"Harvey"*, (1950). Mr Dowd imagined that he had an erstwhile companion, Harvey, a six foot rabbit. But he was the only one who could "see" Harvey. It was not long before other people began to consider the affable Mr Dowd as weird.

The comedy of errors began when his sister, Veta Louise Simmons (played by Josephine Hull), wanted to commit him to a mental institution. The psychiatrist, Doctor Chumley (Cecil Kellaway) found that there was magic and method behind the madness of Elwood P Dowd.

Tom Hanks had the "misfortune" to be born at the "wrong" hour of 11.17 am. The sun was about to reach its peak position in the sky. His ㄒ Ding fire was not needed during the bright hours of the day.

In order to make the comparison between Bruce Boxleitner and Tom Hanks as close as possible, we had to choose two persons who were in the same industry, the same sex and preferably contemporaries.

Who had the greater achievement? Both persons found success but there are varying degrees of success. It would be safe to say that most of the film going public would consider Tom Hanks as the more versatile and greater actor than Bruce Boxleitner.

But this conclusion would go against the theory of the fire hour. To recap, Bruce Boxleitner was born at 4.40 am before the sunrise whereas Tom Hanks was born at 11.17 am when the sun was shining brightly.

How did proponents of the fire theory explain why someone born at the "right" hour had less achievement compared to another person born during the "wrong" hour?

We could have gone on to examine some more charts but ten charts should be sufficient as a sample of charts. We have deliberately stopped at ten because the number ten represented completion in *feng shui*.

We have looked briefly at the charts of four 丙 Bing fire day masters and four 丁 Ding fire day masters. Then we compared the charts of two 丁 Ding fire day masters.

To cast the net as wide as possible, we chose both males and females as well as people from different occupations and nationalities. Only two of the cast of characters hailed from the corporate world.

The proponents of the theory of the fire hour could choose to remain steadfast to their theory. But perhaps they should also try to explain why there seemed to be so many exceptions to their rule. They seemed to have interpreted the symbolism of fire too literally.

There were other ways to interpret why the 丙 Bing fire or 丁 Ding fire day master had achievements despite being born during the "wrong" hours.

But in order to explain these other methods of how to assess whether fire day masters had potential for achievement, we would need to go into more technical detail.

As this article was meant for the beginner reader, perhaps it was not appropriate to explain these technicalities here. It would be more suitable if we delved deeper into technical explanations during a *Ba Zi* course. Another alternative might be to write a book aimed for readers who had some grounding in the subject.

CHAPTER TEN
HELP! WHAT TO DO IF I HAVE AN UNFAVOURABLE BIRTH CHART?

In the study of *Ba Zi*, the student has often been told that when he analysed birth charts for the male, he should concentrate on the wealth element.

Conversely, when he examined birth charts for the female, he should look for the husband and children elements.

The reason was that the male was expected to support the family while the female had to seek a husband and bear children so that she could fulfil her destiny.

Help!

John Lennon & Paul McCartney

Help! I need some-bod-y Help! Not just any - bo-d - y

In that case, it should have been relatively easy to determine whether a person was rich or poor. The element that was controlled by the day master was said to be the wealth element.

If the day master was 丁 Ding fire, then fire controlled metal. Therefore, both 庚 Geng metal and 辛 Xin metal were considered as his wealth.

According to one well-known school of *Phat Chee*, if the chart had many wealth stars, then the person was rich.

This was a misguided concept. It was actually the other way round. The wealthy person usually had only a few wealth stars in his chart.

This brought us to the question, what would happen if a person did not have any wealth stars in his birth chart?

Let us find out by examining the birth charts of two male persons who did not have any wealth elements in their chart.

If there were no wealth stars, did it imply that there would be no wealth? Furthermore, did it also indicate that the person was not only poor, he would probably remain mired in poverty all his life?

PART ONE: THE MEN WHO HAD NO WEALTH STARS IN THEIR CHARTS

To make the comparison as close as possible, we have chosen two charts with the same day master. They shared the same 丁 Ding fire day master. Since fire controlled metal, the wealth element was metal. There was not a single piece of metal in their charts!

MALE #1 13 July 1942

时 Hour		日 Day	月 Month			年 Year	
丙 Bing Fire		丁 Ding Fire	丁 Ding Fire			壬 Ren Water	
午 Wu Horse		卯 Mao Rabbit	未 Wei Goat			午 Wu Horse	
丁 Ding Fire	己 Ji Earth	乙 Yi Wood	己 Ji Earth	丁 Ding Fire	乙 Yi Wood	丁 Ding Fire	己 Ji Earth

MALE #2 21 July 1948

时Hour		日Day			月Month			年Year
丙 Bing Fire		丁 Ding Fire			己 Ji Earth			戊 Wu Earth
午 Wu Horse		未 Wei Goat			未 Wei Goat			子 Zi Rat
丁 Ding Fire	己 Ji Earth	己 Ji Earth	丁 Ding Fire	乙 Yi Wood	己 Ji Earth	丁 Ding Fire	乙 Yi Wood	癸 Gui Water

But these two charts belonged to people who became famous and wealthy. In fact, the proprietor of the second chart became so disenchanted with his material success that he turned to religion and even auctioned off many of his material possessions!

Who were these people? The first chart was that of Harrison Ford.

He was born at 11.41 am, which was the "wrong" hour for a 丁 Ding fire day master.

In 1977, he became the mercenary Hans Solo who fell in love with Princess Leia in *"Star Wars"*. By 1989, he had appeared in the third Indian Jones movie, *"Indiana Jones and the Last Crusade."* In this film, he had to search for the Holy Grail and rescue his father at the same time, the elderly Henry Jones, played by Sean Connery.

As Sean Connery grew older, he would be more frequently cast as an elderly mentor to younger heroes. Perhaps the most memorable of these roles was when he became Allan Quartermain, the mentor to Tom Sawyer (played by Shane West) in *"The League of Extraordinary Gentlemen"* (2003).

The second chart belonged to a rather obscure person by the name of Steven Demetri Georgiou.

This chart was also another 丁 Ding fire day master who was born at the "wrong" hour. Steven Demetri Georgiou had the misfortune to be born at 12.00 pm.

Since it was noon, the sun reached its peak position in the sky. There was no opportunity for the poor 丁 Ding fire to be seen or appreciated in the bright daylight hours.

But Steven Georgiou would find fame and fortune as Cat Stevens. He became a Muslim and adopted the name, Yusef Islam. By 1981, he had grown disenchanted of the material world. He auctioned off many of his material possessions, including his gold records.

Surely it would be futile to deny that Harrison Ford and Cat Stevens had achievements in their lives. How to explain why these two persons had charts which did not contain a single wealth star?

The supporters of the theory that the more wealth stars there were, the richer the person could choose to remain faithful to their concept. But they should also try to explain why there were so many glaring exceptions to their rule.

Therefore, if a person had a supposedly "bad" birth chart, he did not need to fret unduly. There were other ways to interpret a so called bad chart.

However, we would need to go into greater technical detail in order to explain these methods. We do not propose to do so in this book.

PART TWO: THE MYTH OF THE BALANCED CHART

In the study of *Ba Zi*, many schools have taught that the ideal birth chart was the balanced chart. But this seemed to be some romantic ideal, impossible to achieve in real life. Instead, most people had some sort of imbalance in their charts, ranging from mild imbalance of the five elements to seriously imbalanced.

We proposed to show some birth charts which were grossly imbalanced, yet these persons had achievements in life. The imbalance was usually in favour of one particular element at the expense of the other elements.

Female #1 8 March 1922

时Hour	日Day	月Month	年Year
戊 Wu Earth	乙 Yi Wood	癸 Gui Water	壬 Ren Water
寅 Yin Tiger	亥 Hai Pig	卯 Mao Rabbit	戌 Xu Dog
甲　丙　戊 Jia　Bing　Wu Wood　Fire　Earth	壬　甲 Ren　Jia Water　Wood	乙 Yi Wood	戊　辛　丁 Wu　Xin　Ding Earth　Metal　Fire

This female was a 乙 Yi wood day master born in the spring season. Since the 卯 Rabbit month was the peak of spring, this meant that her wood day master was very strong.

There was also a wood combination in her chart. The combinations may be shown as follows:-

寅 Tiger (hour) + 卯 Rabbit (month)
= Seasonal combination of 木 wood

寅 Tiger (hour) + 亥 Pig (day) = Six combination of 木 wood

卯 Rabbit (month) + 亥 Pig (day)
= Three Harmony combination of 木 wood

These combinations made the already strong wood element even stronger. Therefore, we could interpret that this chart was an imbalanced chart in favor of wood. The antithesis of wood was metal. The metal element was rather weak. It was found only in the 戌 Dog year of birth.

Despite this imbalance in her chart, Tula Ellice Finklea would find fame and fortune as a dancer and actress. She was given the stage name of Cyd Charisse and had the opportunity to dance with the most sought after male dancers of her era.

In 1946, she appeared with Fred Astaire in *"Ziegfeld Follies."* But she got her break only in 1952 when she was chosen to dance with Gene Kelly in *"Singing in the Rain."* She followed this up in 1954 by appearing in *"Brigadoon"*, again with Gene Kelly.

She reunited to dance with the demanding Fred Astaire in *"The Band Wagon"* (1951) and *"Silk Stockings"* (1956).

By the time that Cyd Charisse became the dancing partner of Fred Astaire, he had already made most of his dancing films with his erstwhile dancing companion, Ginger Rogers, during the 1930s.

Let us examine a chart that was strong in metal.

Female #2 27 August 1932

时Hour	日Day	月Month	年Year
丁 Ding Fire	庚 Geng Metal	戊 Wu Earth	壬 Ren Water
丑 Chou Ox	申 Shen Monkey	申 Shen Monkey	申 Shen Monkey
己 癸 辛 Ji Gui Xin Earth Water Metal	庚 壬 戊 Geng Ren Wu Metal Water Earth	庚 壬 戊 Geng Ren Wu Metal Water Earth	庚 壬 戊 Geng Ren Wu Metal Water Earth

This second female chart was quite easy to read. She was a 庚 Geng metal day master born in the 申 Monkey month. This meant that her metal was born in season.

There were no combinations in her Earthly Branches. The metal element was repeated in each of her three 甲 Monkeys but they did not form a combination.

There was further metal Qi found in her 丑 Ox hour of birth. But the metal energy was in the tomb when it was located in the 丑 Ox. Therefore, the presence of this metal energy was not so material to the overall structure of her chart.

This chart was evidently imbalanced. It was overly strong in metal. The opposite energy of metal was wood. There was not a single piece of wood in her chart.

To a metal day master, the wood represented her wealth. Since there was no wood, theoretically this person should have been destitute.

In real life, she was far from being poor. She was not only financially independent, she married men who became prominent and could evidently provide for her.

According to theory, imbalanced charts such as this example should not have any potential for achievement. But Antonia Fraser earned a reputation for writing historical biographies and some detective fiction.

In 1969, Lady Fraser won accolades for her magnum opus, *"Mary, Queen of Scots."* She was also able to marry men of high standing in society. Her first husband was Hugh Fraser, a Member of Parliament, whom she married in 1956. They divorced in 1977. There were six children from this marriage.

In 1980, she married the famous playwright, Harold Pinter. They remained married until his death in 2008. Some of Harold Pinter's most significant plays were *"The Birthday Party"*, *"The Room"* and *"The Homecoming."* He won the Nobel Prize for Literature in 2005.

THE ABSTRUSE FIELD OF HISTORICAL WRITING

Traditionally, the field of historical writing, particularly military history and historical biography had been dominated by male writers.

Apart from Lady Antonia Fraser, to the best of our knowledge, there were only two other female writers who excelled in this intricate field.

One of these were her British rival writer, Claire Tomalin. The other writer came from across the Atlantic, an American writer named Barbara Tuchman.

Claire Tomalin was known for her in depth studies of literary figures such as Charles Dickens, Jane Austen and Thomas Hardy. As she was born in 1933, she was a closer contemporary of Lady Fraser. Barbara Tuchman was born in 1912, about two decades earlier than the other two women writers.

Barbara Tuchman's study of General Vinegar Joe Stilwell and the American involvement in China during the Second World War has remained unsurpassed. When the book was first published in 1971, the full title was *"Sand against the Wind: Stilwell and the American experience in China 1911-1945."* Sadly, her publisher, Macmillan, has found this to be a mouthful and have deleted the first four words from the title.

Barbara Tuchman found her métier in her studies of military and political history. Her works such as *"The Guns of August"* (1962) and *"The Proud Tower"* (1966) still remain classics.

Even a lesser known work such as *"The First Salute"* (1988) showed her masterly abilities both as a scholar and a writer with a flair for history. On 16 November 1776, a ship flying the flag of the new Continental Congress entered the port of Saint Eustatius in the West Indies. The ship fired a salute and the guns of the fort returned the salute. It was the first time that any country had fired a salute in recognition of the fledging United States.

If the imbalanced charts were "bad" charts, how could supporters of this theory explain why there were so many imbalanced charts, yet the persons concerned had achievements?

The other commonly held fallacy was that a chart which had many clashes and punishments was a "bad" chart. Let us examine briefly a chart which had two pairs of clashes.

Female #3 12 March 1946

时 Hour			日 Day	月 Month	年 Year		
庚 Geng Metal			乙 Yi Wood	辛 Xin Metal	丙 Bing Fire		
辰 Chen Dragon			酉 You Rooster	卯 Mao Rabbit	戌 Xu Dog		
戊 Wu Earth	乙 Yi Wood	癸 Gui Water	辛 Xin Metal	乙 Yi Wood	戊 Wu Earth	辛 Xin Metal	丁 Ding Fire

This female was also a 乙 Yi wood day master born in the 卯 Rabbit month. Therefore, her wood day master was strong due to being born in season.

There was also a wood combination in her chart.

辰 Dragon (hour) + 卯 Rabbit (month) =
seasonal combination of 木 wood

On the other hand, there was also a metal combination in her chart.

酉 Rooster (day) + 戌 Dog (year)
= partial seasonal combination of 金 metal

This structure already indicated a clash between 木 wood and 金 metal.

As if this clash was not enough, there were two pairs of clashes in her chart.

酉 Rooster (day) + 卯 Rabbit (month) = clash

辰 Dragon (hour) + 戌 Dog (year) = clash

In view of these clashes, it could be argued that this was a "bad" birth chart.

In real life, Liza Minnelli was born to wealthy and famous parents. She was born to Judy Garland and her first husband, film director Vincent Minnelli.

In 1951, her parents divorced. Given her eminent lineage, it seemed inevitable that she should enter show business.

She had a memorable role as Sally Bowles in the musical *"Cabaret"*, (1972). The background of this musical was Germany in the early 1930s, when the Nazi party was about to come into power. *"Cabaret"* was based on a novel, *"The Berlin Stories"* and a play, *"I am a Camera"*, both written by Christopher Isherwood.

However, life was not all roses only for Liza Minnelli. She had to struggle with drug abuse problems. Eventually she checked into the Betty Ford clinic for rehabilitation. However, her problems did not in any way detract from her achievements.

In showing the examples of all these birth charts, we have deliberately omitted the names when we showed the charts to our readers.

The reason was that we did not want our readers to form prejudiced notions about the persons before reading the charts.

For instance, if we knew beforehand that we were reading the chart of a wealthy person, say Steve Jobs, then we would start looking for the wealth aspects. If we did not know that it was the chart of

Steve Jobs, some *Ba Zi* students did not even know how to begin to read the chart!

Therefore, we would like to urge that students of *Ba Zi* should make it a practice to read the chart, not the person behind the chart.

As we can see from the samples of these birth charts, we need not despair if we had supposedly "bad" charts. These "bad" charts could be summarized as follows:-

1. There were no wealth stars in the chart.
2. The charts were grossly imbalanced, overly strong in one or two elements at the expense of the other elements. Sometimes one or more of the other elements were even missing!
3. There were numerous clashes and punishments in the chart.

The proprietors of some of these unfavorable charts had proven that they could not only have achievements in life, these achievements were even remarkable!

Printed in the United States
By Bookmasters